Explore
Niagara-
on-the-Lake

By Susan Walker and Dori Herod

GREEY
dePENCIER
BOOKS

©Greey de Pencier Publications
59 Front Street East
Toronto, Ontario

Printed in Canada 1977

Editor: Claire Gerus
Art Director: Ron Butler
Maps: Franklin Delazzer
Historical Consultant: Francis Petrie, Official Historian to
the City of Niagara Falls

Photo Credits:

Ontario Ministry of Industry and Tourism: 15, 28-29, 31, 65, 71, 75, 79, 87, 91,
96-97, 106, 107, 111, 112-113; Francis Petrie: 4, 11, 12, 13, 16-17, 19, 20, 21, 22,
23, 34, 35, 68-69, 76-77, 116, 118, 119, 120, 121; Toronto Public Library: 18;
Wayne Farrar: 11, 12, 13, 25, 37, 41, 45, 46-47, 51, 53, 55, 59, 61; The Buttery: 32;
Niagara Parks Commission: 13, 103, 108-109; Paul Johns: 42, 43; Fort George:
66; Robert Ragsdale: 79; Shaw Festival: 11, 79, 83; Tom Bochsler: 80, 81;
Preston Haskell: 85; The Oban Inn: 98; The Spectator: 89; The Pillar and
Post: 11, 93; D.N. Chapman: 12; W. McClelland Store: 57.

Cataloguing in Publication Data
Walker, Susan (Date)
   Exploring Niagara-on-the-Lake and the Niagara Peninsula
1. Niagara-on-the-Lake, Ont. — Description — Guide-
books. 2. Niagara Peninsula, Ont. — Description and
travel — Guide-books. I. Herod, Dori (Date)-II. Title.

FC3099.N54A3 1977   971.3'51'044   C77-001281-7
F1059.5.N5W34

ISBN 0-919872-30-1 pa.

Cover Photo — Wayne Farrar

Contents

About the authors

Susan Walker was born in Toronto, educated there and in Boston, and settled along the Niagara River with her husband, a well-known author/physician.

A history enthusiast, she has a special interest in the Niagara area's heritage. She is presently collaborating with Dori Herod on writing fiction with a Niagara setting.

Dori Herod was the original wax artist for Louis Tussaud's Wax Museum in Niagara Falls. Subsequently, she owned and operated "The Merry Muddle" Antique Shop, also in Niagara Falls. She presently sculpts the Dojji wax miniatures listed in the Directory at the back of this book.

Married, with two children, she lives in Niagara-on-the-Lake.

Corner of King and Main Streets
from an old postcard

Foreword

Charm is an elusive quality. We encounter it rarely, so that it is specially prized when it appears.

In this book you will meet a town which has retained the charm of the past. Old Niagara Town was once the seat of government in Upper Canada and the centre of this area's early development. Later, gracious homes, flowering orchards, warm hospitality, pursuit of the arts and a lingering flavor of the past, became part of the town's appeal.

The authors are two women whose friendship I cherish, who are living in or near Niagara town. They share an appreciation of its special qualities and a desire that you, too, will come to know and enjoy it.

If you visit here once, you'll come again. Relax, and be enveloped by the pleasure of discovering Niagara-on-the-Lake.

The Honorable Judy LaMarsh

Elegant Georgian house at 58 Johnson Street

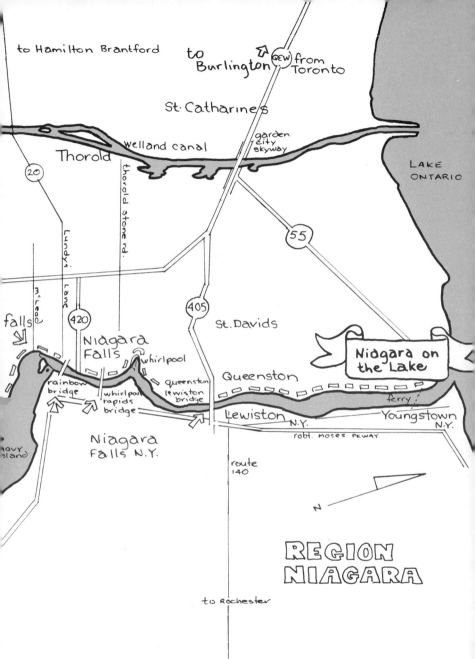

Introduction

How long has it been since you lingered over a breakfast of English muffins and orange marmalade in an elegant country inn? When did you last meander down tree-lined avenues amidst handsome century-old homes with exquisite gardens? Or stroll the grounds of an historic fort imagining the sights and rumblings of a distant past? Does it sound like a picturesque English village? It's on your doorstep in Niagara-on-the-Lake, a peaceful, creative community where the pace of life is casual and easy.

Niagara's natural beauty and gentle climate are conducive to bicycling or walks along the shores of its mighty river, picnics in parks overlooking the lake, sailing, and enjoying the simplicity of the great outdoors. Charming inns offer dining and accommodation in a relaxed atmosphere. Shops abound with original wares, antiques and handicrafts, and some have galleries for browsing and tearooms. Unrivalled entertainment is available in two distinctive theatres, the Mime and the Shaw Festival. All is within easy reach.

The writing of this book originated over a glass of champagne one New Year's Eve. We proposed to compile a practical, commonsense guide to the many facets of our charming town — a book that would help readers discover its unique features. We also hoped that a guidebook documenting some of the town's attractive features might help the inhabitants in their struggle to keep Niagara-on-the Lake as it is.

The government has recently approved plans to pour money into restoration. It is our hope that it will consider carefully the potential for ruin through careless expansion. Niagara-on-the-Lake is a well-loved hideaway, and its people prefer to protect it as such.

In the course of our writing we have received friendly cooperation and met many fascinating people who communicated freely. Space and the infinite amount of material made it impossible for us to include everything.

Special thanks go to Judy La-Marsh, Paul Johns, Franklin Delazzer, Francis Petrie, Donald Combe, and the Niagara Parks Commission.

Susan Walker
Dori Herod
April, 1977

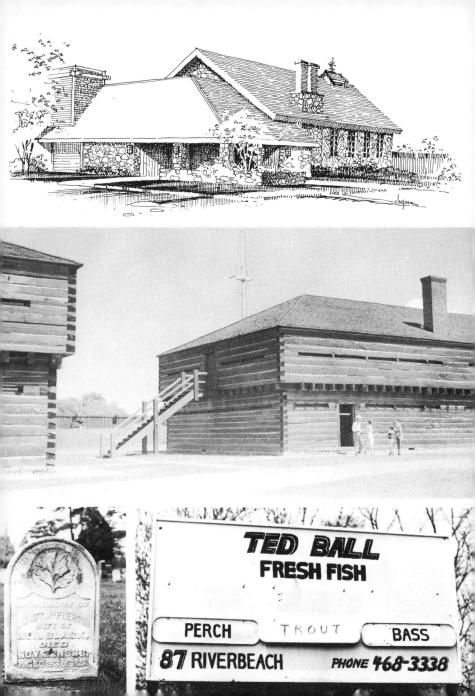

1. How it all began: A historical drama

The year is 1780, and the curtains open on a tranquil wilderness, with wooded hills sloping down to a turbulent river, fertile black soil and a temperate climate.

Enter, a band of peaceful Indians of Iroquois origin, whose territory straddles the Niagara River. Their lives are simple — the women cultivate beans, corn, squash and tobacco; the men hunt and fish. Thirty families live in each of the wooden "long houses" sparsely dotting the wild land.

The Iroquois, occupying most of what is now Western New York, enjoy a settled existence of comparatively sophisticated communal living, and their language and culture are rich and colorful; their lands are vast and productive.

The first white settlers — five Loyalist refugee familes from troubled lands — arrive at Fort Niagara seeking peace and freedom. Driven from their homes in New Jersey, New York, and Pennsylvania by the first skirmishes of the American Revolution, these Loyalists to the Crown have traveled a long and difficult journey by wagon and on foot.

A treaty between England and the Iroquois in 1784 provides a narrow stretch of land for these refugees on each side of the Niagara River from its mouth to the cataract. Here, on the west bank the first settlers take possession of land grants. The men, husbands and fathers, had been members of Butler's Rangers or other regiments fighting for the British Crown in the War of Independence. But, as more refugees begin pouring into the Niagara area, overcrowding at the fort forces them to abandon its security and cross the turbulent river and settle here.

Now begins the arduous task of building log cabins on the uncultivated, lonely shore before the onset of the cold winter months. With the generous aid of the native Indians who freely offer their knowledge of the land, the settlers create primitive gardens and farms on the rich soil.

Soon more pioneers arrive from the United States and England, and Negro slaves seek freedom from their trials in the troubled south. The British Government offers wheat to its frontier families which soon ripens in abundance. The government also builds a few mills to convert the wheat to flour, but their number is inadequate; independent millers — the first businessmen — now appear to answer a growing need for granaries. Log cabins multiply; the community, first

Brock's Monument

14

Battle of Queenston Heights, Oct. 13th, 1813.

Early print of the Battle of Queenston Heights

John Graves Simcoe

called West Niagara, then Butlers-
burg, prospers and swells. By 1786 the
village has grown to nearly 200 inhabitants.

In 1792, a dominant figure enters
the Niagara scene: Colonel John
Graves Simcoe, an aristrocratic military man, Redcoat, scholar, author,
and member of the British House of
Commons. He and his talented wife —
a diarist and artist — are welcomed
joyfully by the settlers as the Lieuten-
ant Governor and wife, the King's
representatives. Under his firm
leadership, the village is named
Newark, capital of Upper Canada.

As the area begins to thrive, Simcoe
divides it into districts, creates a
parliament based on English law,
supports the growth of an agricultural
society, and encourages the presence
of a garrison of British Redcoats for
protection.

A log fort rises to house the soldiers.
But in 1794, a farsighted Governor
Simcoe — fearing the proximity of the
American border — moves the legisla-
ture permanently to York (later
Toronto) before the outbreak of the
war in 1812.

In spite of the move, the land bustles
with military men, merchants, and
skilled craftsmen from Europe who
are called upon to build more sophisticated dwellings — Georgian homes —
at first of wood and later brick. On
Lake Ontario, trading ships bring
construction products to the new land,
and a shipbuilding industry follows on
the river bank. A library, a court
house, an apothecary, and a newspap-
er, all become firsts in Upper Canada.
Justice, peace and contentment pre-
vail.

Suddenly, in October of 1812, the government in Washington orders American soldiers at Lewiston, N.Y., to cross the river, and lay seige to the prosperous community at Queenston. American government officials have observed its growth, as well as the expanse of Crown lands surrounding it, which have become a desirable adjunct to their expanding republic. The British Redcoats, led by their beloved General Isaac Brock, defend the area, but the odds are against them. Brock's militia is dwarfed by the 4,000 American troops under Major-General Stephen Van Rensselaer, and the general population, many of whom emigrated from the American states, is discouraged by the odds against them and reluctant to enter the battle.

On the morning of October 13, General Brock is awakened at Fort George by the sound of cannonfire from the American shore. He dresses, mounts his loyal steed, Alfred, and races off alone towards Queenston to assess the status of his two cannons — one on Vrooman's farm a half mile north of the village and the other on the side of the cliff overlooking the river. He finds that American troops have already achieved the summit of Queenston Heights.

Upon the arrival of his troops, Brock leads a hurried charge up the hill toward the enemy. Driven back, they regroup and charge again. A shot rings out from the brush, a bullet strikes Brock in the chest, and he dies soon after on the battlefield. His men — shocked by the loss of their leader — carry Brock's body from the field to a stone house at the foot of the heights

John Butler

View of the First Brock Monument from Lewiston, 1830. Early print.

A second battle is undertaken in the afternoon, led by Brock's successor, Colonel Roger Sheaffe. The Redcoats march through the bush to the heights behind the enemy's position, and with the help of Indians entrap and defeat the American troops.

Following the battle, Brock's body is carried back to Fort George and is buried three days later while both Redcoats and defeated American soldiers salute him with cannonfire. Thus heralds the beginning of a desperate war that will rage throughout the Niagara peninsula for two more years.

Sheaffe – now a Major-General — takes command and temporarily disperses the invaders. Although Sheaffe will later be awarded a baronetcy for his victory, the martyred Brock is to remain first in the affections of Upper Canada for years to come.

Winter arrives, blurring the countryside with snow, icy blasts and frigid weather. War ceases until spring when Fort George is again assaulted. Red-hot shot fired from the opposite bank illuminates the sky. The fort finally succumbs to flames.

* * * * *

Scene Two finds Newark under the domination of the invading troops. Enemy soldiers inhabit private homes and beautiful St. Mark's Church is converted into a storehouse and hospital. Some of the residents flee to the countryside; others remain to keep the town alive. American soldiers, 2,000 strong, continue their drive westward, forcing 800 British stragglers and loyal Indians as far back as Burlington Heights (now the site of Dundurn Castle in Hamilton), a distance of 35 miles.

In June, the British, returning to

Early print of Laura Secord's home in Queenston; 1894.

Stoney Creek, launch a surprise attack, catching the Americans asleep and unprepared. Hooting and howling on a black night, the small contingent, including Indian supporters, routs the invaders. Waves of ragged soldiers, flushed with victory, move again towards Newark, pushing the enemy into retreat as they go. Throughout summer and fall, cannonfire continues to plague land and lake.

Angered by British use of Indians to aid their cause and Indian tactics in warfare, the Americans loot and burn local villages in their path, taking prisoners and destroying property as they retreat toward Fort George and the river. Winter finds them encamped inside the repaired barricade at Fort George, but fresh British regiments move in and threaten to trap them. When their dwindling numbers force the Americans to abandon the fort, they burn the village of Newark in revenge before their return to the other side of the river. The townspeople are driven into the December snow to watch their homes and possessions go up in flames. When the flames have died, most of Newark has been levelled, including most of Fort George, the churches, and all of the homes but two.

The colonists doggedly begin to rebuild Newark while battles continue elsewhere in the Niagara peninsula at Lundy's Lane, 10 miles away, and in Fort Erie at the southern end of the Niagara River. In 1814, Fort Mississauga is constructed at the river mouth, one-half mile from Fort George, but at that year's end the Treaty of Ghent, signed on Christmas Eve, finally halts a useless war of acquisition, and the new fort never fires a shot.

As peace settles and trade quickens, new clouds gather on the horizon. In

Old powder magazine at Fort George, before and after restoration.

1829, the Welland Canal opens 10 miles west of the Niagara River, running parallel to it from Port Dalhousie to Port Robinson. Four years later it is extended to Port Colborne. Newark's shipping ceases, port facilities fall idle; shipbuilders move elsewhere, and the vitality of the town begins to ebb slowly away.

* * * * *

The third scene opens in 1854, with the town, carrying a new name, Niagara, stubbornly refusing to die. Enter a life-sustaining force at last in the form of a noisy steam locomotive called "The Niagara." Constructed by Samuel Zimmerman, owner of the Clifton Hotel in Niagara Falls and the steamer "Samuel Zimmerman" from Toronto, it is the first steam engine in the area. Iron rails are laid on King Street as far as the wharf in order to connect with the steamship. The locomotive, puffing clouds of black smoke, finally arrives, pulling two rumbling passenger cars and a baggage car. Now, the connections completed between Toronto, Hamilton, Niagara Falls and Niagara-on-the-Lake, the way is open for sightseers and travelers. Gradually the townspeople become used to the train's rumble and the hoot of the steamer, and welcome the tourist trade, constructing elegant waterfront inns and great verandahed and gabled summer homes to house visitors.

Niagara's attractive setting, moderate climate, closeness to metropolitan areas, and historic preservation act as a magnet to attract travelers. Historians, craftsmen and artists settle here and further enrich the town. The land's rich soil supports agriculture and shipbuilders, carpenters and masons contribute their skills to future generations. In 1900 — for postal reasons — another name change distinguishes the locality from Niagara Falls and it becomes the more poetic "Niagara-on-the Lake."

Slowly, the work of the town's restoration begins, with Fort George the first site to be restored by the government in 1937. A host of other great old buildings await their turn: the Court House, churches and the inns.

In the early 1970s, stirrings of another kind of drama begin as the Shaw Festival Theatre and the Canadian Mime theatre develop from the dream of lawyer Brian Doherty. The theatre promises to become the town's life-support system and as others support his concept, an awesome new theatre mushrooms in an open meadow on the edge of town. It is completed in 1973, in time to open its doors to Queen Elizabeth II.

Today, there is renewed interest in restoring the town. Traditional crafts can be seen in a variety of old and new shops and residents take pride in restoring lovely old homes. Hotels are undergoing renovation; sleek yachts can be viewed in the harbor; new theatre groups are beginning to form and citizens are mobilizing to ensure that the tranquility of the town will not be threatened by large commercial chains. The curtain closes with our belief that Niagara-on-the-Lake will continue to be a cultural oasis in a setting of natural beauty.

Monument to Governor and Lady Simcoe, Navy Hall.

2. Walking tour

And now to begin exploring. In this and the next chapter are two tours, one walking and one driving or bicycling, designed to introduce you to Niagara-on-the-Lake. You can walk through the centre of town along Queen, the main street, and make occasional forays down some of the more interesting side streets. By using this walking tour as a framework for your own explorations, you'll see both the commercial area with its shops and the natural waterfront. The time this walk takes is up to you — you could complete it in an hour, or it could take a full day. (We recommend that you put your watch away!)

Let's begin at the Shaw Festival Theatre, one of the newest buildings in town, and end with one of the oldest, the Apothecary.

The Shaw Theatre stands at the junction of Wellington Street and the new Queen's Parade Road, created in 1973 to commemorate the visit of Queen Elizabeth II. The coral brick theatre, designed by architect Ron Thom, was completed barely in time for the Royal Tour that year, and landscaping was still being finished the day of the opening. Although it is one of the few new buildings in town, the theatre does "belong", adding contemporary beauty and pleasing design to a historical environment.

Across Queen's Parade Road, you will see Niagara Hospital, one of Ontario's few surviving small community hospitals, built in 1921 and still serving the medical needs of the town.

Opposite the hospital is St. Vincent de Paul Church. Still in operation, this stucco building was erected in 1834, the first Roman Catholic Church in the Niagara peninsula. Although enlarged in 1965, much of the old Gothic structure was preserved, as evidenced by the long, vertical windows inside and vaulted ceiling with Doric columns for support. Take a moment to browse through the tombstones behind this church — many date back to the 1800s.

Here, too, is the Polish soldiers' burial plot, donated by the church to members of the Polish regiment training in Niagara-on-the-Lake during World War I, who lost their lives during a deadly influenza epidemic. Today many Polish descendants make a pilgrimage each year to the site.

On leaving the cemetery, you will notice the original Moffat Hotel, an old stucco building of the 1830s, unrestored as yet, at 60 Picton St. Beside it in strong contrast is the new Moffat Mews, completed in 1976 to

McCrae Hall

WALKING TOUR

1 Shaw Festival Theatre
2 Niagara Hospital
3 St. Vincent de Paul Church
4 Moffat Hotel
5 Moffat Mews
6 Marianne's Fabrics
7 Colonial Fudge
8 Peanut Mill
9 Prince of Wales Hotel
10 Simcoe Park
11 The Clocktower
12 Niagara Apothecary
13 Old Niagara Book Shop
14 Brassbound's Cafe
15 The Buttery
16 The Sign of the Pineapple
17 Old Court House
18 Greaves Jams and Jellies
19 Howe's Antiques
20 McCrae Hall
21 Royal George Theatre
22 Bank of Montreal
23 Grace United Church
24 McClelland's West End Store
25 Gate House
26 Rogers-Harrison House
27 MacDougal-Harrison House
28 Crysler-Rigg House
29 Golf Course
30 Fort Mississauga
31 Oban Inn
32 Kirby House
33 Queen's Royal Park
34 Whale Inn
35 Masonic Hall
36 The Rectory
37 St. Mark's Church
38 Campbell-Scott House
39 American Inn
40 Riverside Inn
41 Canada Customs House
42 Gillingham's Yacht Basin

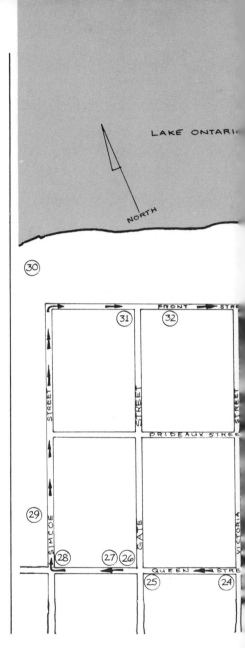

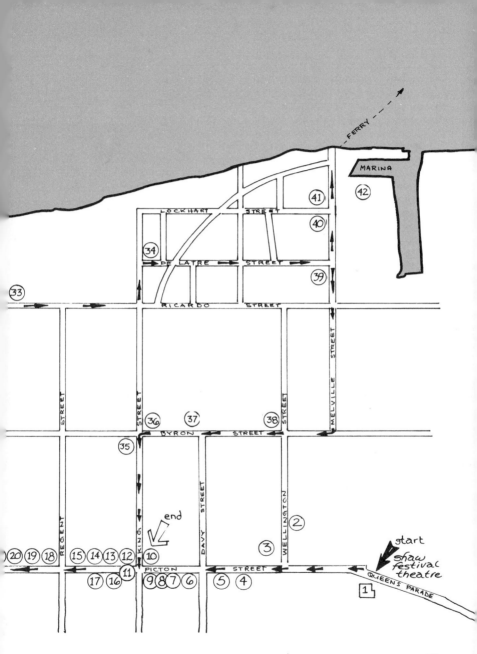

LOCKHART STREET

DE LATRE STREET

RICARDO STREET

BYRON STREET

PICTON STREET

MARINA

FERRY

MELVILLE STREET

WELLINGTON STREET

DAVY STREET

KING STREET

REGENT STREET

STREET

end

start
shaw
festival
theatre

QUEENS PARADE

27

house shops with a 19th century flavor, including a candlemaker, a clockmaker, two restaurants, and a travel service.

Further along Picton, at No. 24, Marianne's Fabrics and Colonial Fudge share an old building. Next door, the Peanut Mill, a natural foods store, offers freshly ground peanut butter, herbal teas, vitamins and granola.

The red and gold Prince of Wales Hotel stands at the corner of Picton and King Streets. Built in the late 1800s, and later named in honor of the Prince's visit to Canada, its ornate gingerbread facade and new addition enclose 40 rooms, dining room, bar and banquet rooms. The inviting glass Garden Room encourages guests to linger for lunch, dinner or refreshments with a view of the happenings in Simcoe Park across the street.

This park, bordering the grounds of St. Vincent de Paul Church, offers lovely green lawns, a children's playground, a wading pool, picnic areas, and other local outdoor activities. Sunday afternoon concerts in summer begin at 2 p.m., with local bands providing music. Visitors often stop for information at the information booth at the edge of the park.

Here, at the corner of King, Picton becomes Queen Street, dominated from this view by the famous clocktower in the middle of the road. This memorial, donated by the Royal Canadian Legion to the martyrs of World War I, created a great deal of controversy among town residents, who opposed its location, design, and

Clock Tower on Queen Street

cost. The monument was finally accepted and dedicated in 1922. The controversy, however, has continued even into recent years: when plays were first being staged in the Court House Theatre, the clock's chimes — housed within the building — became a nuisance. The chimes were eventually muffled while performances were in progress, but the problem still exists and new solutions are being considered.

The battery-operated clock inside the tower is maintained and repaired by Jim Henry, a local electrician, as a labor of love. In order to master its complex inner workings, Jim has had to experiment and improvise because the original was purchased in England 53 years ago and parts are irreplaceable. Batteries must be replaced twice a year and gears require hand winding.

On the north side of Queen Street, near the tower, is the Niagara Apothecary, the oldest pharmacy in Upper Canada. It was open from 1866 to 1964, when the Niagara Foundation bought it and restored it to its original state. The Golden Mortar — traditional sign of the pharmacy — is still on display, as well as the chemist's "show globes," original walnut counters and chandeliers. The Apothecary no longer has items for sale, but is open to tourists as an historic attraction in the spring and summer.

Next door, you'll find the Old Niagara Book Shop — a bookstore with a difference. It occupies a recently decorated old house, with books artfully displayed on round tables for browsing, and, because of the artistic and historical bent of the community, offers an excellent selection of art books and Canadiana.

Both Brassbound's Café and the Buttery — two restaurants of long standing in Niagara — are owned by the same friendly couple, the Niemanns. Brassbound's offers quick lunches and snacks; the Buttery, more elegant fare. Drinks and teas on the Buttery's outdoor verandah in warm weather offers a welcome interlude for visitors and residents alike.

On the south side of Queen, across from the Buttery, The Sign of the Pineapple looms tall and yellow. Originally a grocery store in the 1830s, it now houses an interesting variety of antiques and gifts.

The old grey stone Court House stands solemnly on the same side of the street, designed in 1847 by the esteemed William Thomas, whose firm also created the St. Lawrence Hall in Toronto and the Halifax Court House. A large cupola, later removed, gave it prominence on the street, the building replaced the first town Court House and housed the last remaining government officials after the capital had been moved to York. Today it houses the public library at the rear and a small summer theatre, and stoically awaits restoration.

A whiff of Greaves Jams and Jellies will meet you at 55 Queen St. Operated since 1928 by the Greaves family, their tasty fruit products can be purchased on site in this 100-year-old building. Moving along, you'll pass Howe's Antiques at No. 61, a small but distinctive shop, and McCrae Hall at No. 65, a gift shop of

The Sign of the Pineapple antique store

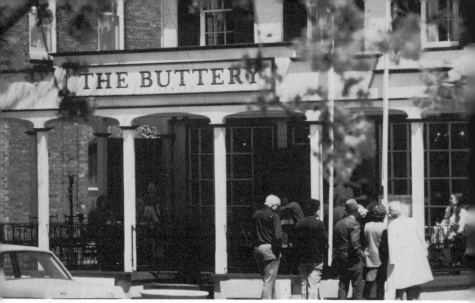

The Buttery's verandah, a pleasant place for tea

quality where afternoon tea is served on delicate china. Next, the Royal George Mime Theatre's new facade gleams like a polished gem. Converted from a movie house in 1974 by restoration architect Peter John Stokes, it boasts a Georgian facade, a spiral staircase in the lobby, and the traditional mime décor of black and white.

At Victoria Street and Queen's south side, abutting the sidewalk, you will be struck by the solidity of Grace United Church, another William Thomas design, in 1852. In contrast to the church, you may wonder at the aged and slightly crooked appearance of McClelland's grocery store. Pause here for a look at the sloping interior of the old shop, where you can purchase a slab or two of their excellent cheeses. This store has been in the same location since 1873, but the building itself is even older. Look for the sign over the doorway — a large T — the traditional sign of sellers of tea.

At the next corner of the same block you'll reach the Gate House with its yellow canopy. If the day is warm and your legs are weary, this might be a good place to stop for a cool drink on the front verandah, where you can look across the golf course to Lake Ontario.

Crossing Queen Street and following its north side to Simcoe Street you will pass three historic houses, still used as dwellings. The Rogers-Harrison house at 157 Queen St. was built of stucco, cut and lined to resemble stone. With its shutters, fanlight and sidelighted doorway close to the sidewalk, it is Georgian in style, although the door is off centre. Built about 1823, its original owners were among the first residents in Niagara and thus able to locate a fine home in the centre of town.

The MacDougal-Harrison house next door was erected at approximately the same time. An example of the early row house style used in Niagara, the brick grouping features arcaded windows, a side hall plan, and an original doorway with elaborate fanlight and sidelights. Its most famous inhabitant was Colonel Daniel Mac Dougal, who fought and was wounded in the battle of Lundy's Lane.

At 187 Queen St., Ralph Crysler built his home in the 1820s. Its substantial, two-storey clapboard dwelling displays the symmetry of balanced shuttered windows and fluted pilasters. Although many changes and additions have been made to this house, including a turn-of-the-century verandah, the original carpenter's skill is still visible in the elaborate cornices. Dr. Rigg, the local physician who presently owns the house, has cultivated at the rear a garden well-known to residents.

Leave Queen Street now and travel north on Simcoe towards the lake two blocks away. On your left is the golf course, and standing at the edge in the distance is Fort Mississauga. This structure has been fenced off to protect it until restoration takes place at some future date. It was erected during the War of 1812, but has since been battered by the elements and fallen to ruins. Plans are in the initial stage to rebuild its unique star formation and the embattlements surrounding it.

A turn to the right on Front Street brings you alongside the river bank and the Oban Inn at Front and Gate Streets. The Oban was originally a private home, built in 1824 by a river captain, and was later converted to an inn. Today it is popular with tourists and local residents for its friendly appeal and good food.

Continuing along Front Street, you'll pass the Kirby House at No. 130, with a plaque in front declaring that William Kirby, author, lived here from 1857. The house is much older, probably dating from 1818, and many alterations have been made, but the stucco finish, central doorway, and balanced windows remain as they were originally.

Front Street will bring you to Queen's Royal Park where once stood a gracious Inn, demolished in 1929. Here is an especially good view of the somber Fort Niagara guarding the American shore and the mouth of the Niagara river. (Read more about this fort in the Youngstown-Lewiston section further on in this book.)

Turn left on King Street, following the hill down toward Delatre Street and the Whale Inn at the bottom. Built in 1835 to accommodate sailors and travelers arriving at the dock, it features a central hall plan, shuttered windows and pilastered doorway and is now a private home.

At the end of Delatre Street you come to Gillingham's Yacht Basin, with the small white Canada Customs House on the dock to the left. Here the ferry from Youngstown, N.Y., lands and visitors coming from the United States must pass inspection.

A climb up Melville Street two blocks to Byron brings you back to the hospital again, with the nurses' resi-

The Apothecary in 1914...

dence in front of you. Now, turn right on Byron, noting the modern cedarboard home of Campbell Scott at No. 89. This is another example of modern architecture in an old town which gently adds a contemporary influence.

Pass Wellington Street and look for St. Mark's Church nestled among the trees on the right. The rectangular stone church, opened around 1804, was one of the first parishes in Upper Canada. Used as a hospital and barracks during the War of 1812, it survived the destructive fire and was enlarged to its cruciform shape in 1834. The churchyard cemetery contains the tombstones of many of Niagara's first settlers, as it was the only burial site and therefore used by all denominations in early years.

The yellow brick rectory beside the church dates back to 1858, and was fashioned to resemble a Tuscan villa. Its square tower, wide eaves and massive trim are typical of mid-

century Italian architecture, and a special feature of this building is a spiral staircase rising from the central hall.

From the sidewalk in front of the rectory, you can see a white stucco building with black shutters on the diagonal corner at King Street. Originally a barracks, this was the site of the first Masons' meeting in Upper Canada in 1792. The Ontario Heritage Foundation has designated this building a historic site and it is the only private building in Ontario so honored.

At King and Queen Streets, you can return to the Apothecary, a good place to end your tour and look for an old-fashioned cure for tired feet!

*... and today. A museum well worth a
visit.*

3. Driving or bicycling tour

Within the tiny boundaries of Niagara-on-the-Lake you'll find the largest number of occupied late Georgian houses in Canada.

A natural product of the order and reason of the 18th century, Georgian architecture originated during the reigns of Britain's first three King Georges. The Loyalist settlers arriving in Upper Canada brought with them both a love of freedom, and a desire for harmony and balance. These qualities were reflected in their homes.

The basic Georgian-style home was a rectangular building with the entrance in the centre front, a central hall, balanced windows, and a dominant doorway crowned by a fan-shaped window to emphasize the hospitality of the owner. As the basic design improved, variations appeared, softening the original stern appearance.

Most of the early Georgian homes in Niagara were destroyed by fire during the War of 1812. The homes which were built later were characterized by a scaling down of trim, more delicate detail, larger windows and carved mantels. Stucco often replaced the earlier clapboard and brick, columns were reduced to pilasters, and staircases began to curve gently. The overall effect was one of less weight and more eloquent detail.

Some of Niagara's old homes have survived numerous physical moves from one location to another. The Crook-Johns house, for example, has endured three major moves. Built by James Crook in 1826, it was moved from Johnson and King Streets to Simcoe and Queen when it changed owners. This was a long, tedious affair involving rollers, a winch and horses. Upon the next transfer of occupant in 1907, it became the Campbell house and was resituated at Queen and Victoria Streets. There it was purchased by its present owner, Paul Johns, who relocated the home at 280 Dorchester St. in the fall of 1975, where he restored and enhanced it inside and out. (Note: Although out of range of our driving tour map, it's within the town limits and worth a look.

You can see several of Niagara-on-the-Lake's historic homes by driving, bicycling, or walking parts of the following tour. Bicycles are for rent at the Pillar and Post Inn, and sometimes at other locations in town. Visit the information booth in Simcoe Park for more information on bicycle rentals.

(Every year the Niagara Founda-

Post House

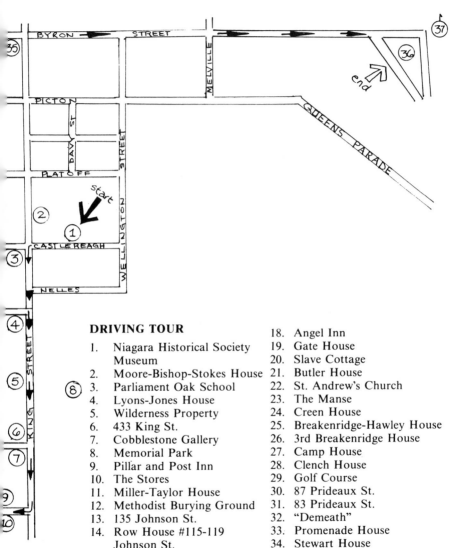

DRIVING TOUR

1. Niagara Historical Society Museum
2. Moore-Bishop-Stokes House
3. Parliament Oak School
4. Lyons-Jones House
5. Wilderness Property
6. 433 King St.
7. Cobblestone Gallery
8. Memorial Park
9. Pillar and Post Inn
10. The Stores
11. Miller-Taylor House
12. Methodist Burying Ground
13. 135 Johnson St.
14. Row House #115-119 Johnson St.
15. 95 Johnson St.
16. 96 Johnson St.
17. 58 Johnson St.
18. Angel Inn
19. Gate House
20. Slave Cottage
21. Butler House
22. St. Andrew's Church
23. The Manse
24. Creen House
25. Breakenridge-Hawley House
26. 3rd Breakenridge House
27. Camp House
28. Clench House
29. Golf Course
30. 87 Prideaux St.
31. 83 Prideaux St.
32. "Demeath"
33. Promenade House
34. Stewart House
35. 18 Prideaux St.
36. Fort George
37. Navy Hall

tion provides an annual tour of private homes on the last Saturday in May. Because this event is so popular bookings must be procured well in advance. Write to the Niagara Foundation, Niagara-on-the-Lake, Ont. for reservations.)

A good starting point is the Niagara Historical Society Museum at Castlereagh Street, where you can visually absorb some of the area's history for a better understanding of the tour ahead. Brochures and pamphlets are available here; admission is $1 for adults, 50¢ for children. The museum is open afternoons only; daily in summer and Wednesday, Friday and Saturday in winter.

After leaving the Museum, follow right along Castlereagh to King, where, if you pause at the corner, you can see a yellow house one block down on the right. Known as the Moore-Bishop-Stokes house (c. 1828) it's an early example of Georgian architecture, although it has been somewhat altered by a succession of owners. A refreshing example of a colonial home painted other than white, it is owned by Peter John Stokes, the architect-author of "Old Niagara on the Lake," a book of histories and sketches of historic local houses.

Continue south along King Street, watching for Parliament Oak School on the right, so named for the fact that Governor Simcoe held one of the first meetings of Parliament under a spreading oak tree on this property.

At the corner of Centre and King Streets, at 8 Centre St., is the Lyons-Jones house (c. 1835), a small Regency house differing from the Georgian style by its position back from the road, its white stucco and its side hall plan. Nevertheless, the Georgian symmetry, shutters and fanlight windows are still present, although the shuttered windows to the left of the door are blind, a Regency "deceit."

Right next door is the Wilderness property, a large treed lot given by the Indians to the widow of Daniel Claus, their agent. The house, barely visible in summer from King Street, was built by the agent's son, William, in 1816. It is a low stucco cottage with lines cut to resemble stone, shuttered, with a centre hall plan. A huge oak reputed to be the oldest in Southern Ontario and cared for by public funds still stands on the lush wooded grounds. At one time several oaks on this property were landmarks for navigators on the lake.

At 433 King St., beside the Wilderness property, is another old house dating from General Brock's era. Now stucco, the house has undergone many alterations, but enjoys the reputation of once having lodged Brock's fiancée, who often welcomed the General as a visitor to its hearth.

Stop at the corner of King and Mary Streets and visit the Cobblestone Gallery at 463 King St. Canadian paintings are for sale here, exhibited in the warm glow of an old house. Some of the artists represented are James Kierstead, Ken Hanson and Campbell Scott.

On your way out of the gallery, look across King to Butler's Barracks in the distance. Built in 1778, it is believed to

Top: Johnson Street row houses
Bottom: Crook -Johns House

Slave Cottage

be one of the oldest buildings in the town, originally housing Butler's Rangers. These men — loyal to the British Crown — carried on guerilla warfare against the rebellious Americans during the War of Independence. At the time of writing, the barracks were undergoing renovation by Parks Canada as an historic site and were not open to the public.

Continue up King to John Street, and turn right to arrive at The Pillar and Post Inn. The old part of the complex, the Arts and Handcraft Shop, faces John Street and was originally built as a cannery. You'll be drawn to the beautifully displayed crafts and unusual merchandise. On John Street across from the Inn is a favorite shop for boating enthusiasts, "The Stores." Turn right to Regent from John Street and look for the small, neat Miller-Taylor house at 46

Mary St. Built around 1817 and typical of the very earliest Georgian construction, it is symmetrical and simple, almost barren of detail. Take a left on Mary to Gate Street, two blocks away, then follow Gate two blocks to the Methodist Burial Ground which dates from 1822. After you've looked around a bit, go down another block to Johnson Street, where a right turn will bring you to several interesting historic homes.

On your left at No. 135 is a balanced, simple, white Georgian frame dwelling, shuttered, with its doorway unadorned and close to the road. On the same side, at 115 to 119 Johnson St. are three Georgian row houses painted dark red, also very simple and unadorned. These provided small living quarters for workers and suggest that there may have been other such groupings elsewhere in the

Promenade House

town. On the corner of Victoria and Johnson Streets at No. 95 stands the red brick Post House, inscribed with the date 1835 over the white door. This solid brick, black-shuttered home is late Georgian, and belonged to the town's postmaster. Its dignified exterior reflects the stature and esteem accorded the postmaster at that time. Look for a discoloration of the bricks at the left front corner of the building, revealing that a door once existed here for townspeople to pick up mail.

Across the street from the Post House, at No. 96, rests a restored white frame dwelling with black shutters dating from the period immediately after the War of 1812.

Moving along to the corner of Johnson and Regent Streets, you can look at 58 Johnson St., another elegant Georgian house, built close to the road, with a finely trimmed

doorway, pilasters, fanlight and sidelights. An interesting feature of this house is the interior chimney with fireplaces set in the inner corners of the front rooms, a practical solution to keeping warm in Canadian winters. The house has been restored and enlarged.

Turn left at Regent Street down to Market Street and the Angel Inn on the corner. Its mellowed halls offer a warm feeling of early Canadian life. Dating from the mid-1820s, rough-hewn beams and shuttered windows, pine tables and a glowing fire invite you to settle in for lunch or dinner in the cozy dining rooms.

Then, head back to Queen Street, a block away; turn left and travel two blocks to Gate Street, take another left beside the Gate House, and begin another loop through the southwest section of town.

At the corner of Gate and Johnson Streets, notice the tiny white "slave cottage" on the right. Typical of the early cottages often used by slaves, this contains two rooms and a steep, narrow staircase to an upper loft. It has been restored, with the framework, floors, and much interior woodwork still in the original materials.

Right on Johnson to Simcoe, and left on Simcoe, brings you to Butler House (c. 1817), a grey stucco with a bright yellow door, halfway up the block at No. 275. Set originally on Butler farmland west of town, the house was moved into the village and restored, with many of its original features still intact, including the centre hall plan, its shuttered windows and uniform facade.

On the next block on Simcoe Street, set apart in splendid isolation, is lovely St. Andrew's Church. Built in 1831, restored in 1937, its basic rectangular shape offers stability, while delicate trim and rising Doric columns create a graceful dignity. At the same time the crowning tower and spire lend an air of English tradition.

Across the street at Simcoe and Centre Streets, is St. Andrew's Rectory, a single-storey, pink brick Georgian manse. Built in 1836, it once housed runaway slaves in the basement. It has recently been restored.

John Breakenridge, a prominent barrister in town, constructed a home at 363 Simcoe St. during the years 1817-25. Thomas Creen, the first rector of St. Mark's moved in, and it became known as the Creen House, with Reverend Creen at one time holding school here. The building has now been restored closely to the original and painted pale yellow.

Right around the corner at 392 William St., is the white clapboard Breakenridge-Hawley house fronting on Mississauga Street. Built in 1818, this was Breakenridge's second house, now beautifully restored to its original grandeur. The balanced shuttered windows frame a doorway decorated with fluted pilasters, crowned with Ionic capitals. Unlike its contemporaries, the house is set well back from the road. Look for the coach house to the rear, which the present owners have preserved to complement the house. The owner, Frank Hawley, is chairman of the Niagara Foundation, dedicated to restoring historical sites.

Breakenridge built a third time on this block, at 240 Centre St., one block to the right. This house was much plainer than the second, but made of brick, with more fireplaces and easier to heat. Its doorway was unadorned, compared with the Breakenridge-Hawley house. When Breakenridge died in 1828, he left the house to his wife, who ran a school in it for a few years. Today, it still awaits restoration.

Continuing along Mississauga, past St. Andrew's churchyard with its interesting old headstones, you'll see the yellow stucco Camp House at the head of Gage Street, on the left side of the road. Built about 1818, it was once a busy private school known as Dr. Whitelaw's. It is shutterless, with no fanlight, and built close to the road.

Johnson Street is the site of Clench House at No. 234. One of the best examples of a wealthy Loyalist family dwelling, it was built by an officer of

234 Johnson St.

Butler's Rangers who later rose to political distinction. This frame house, dating to the 1820s, has a centre hall plan and is gable shaped with all the Georgian trim. The front offers an impressive facade of five bays between fluted pilasters, and a centre doorway with fanlight and sidelights.

At the next block, a left turn takes you back to Queen Street; the golf course can be seen across Queen to the left, with Fort Mississauga awaiting restoration on the grounds.

Cross Queen Street and follow Simcoe Street one more block to Prideaux for a glimpse of historic homes in the old part of town. Take a right at Prideaux to Gate and Victoria Streets. Within this block are four houses of note: 87 Prideaux St., a small white stucco with grey shutters and a side hall plan; at 83, a small

white frame house with centre hall, also with grey shutters and built on the roadside, contrasts with the more substantial "Demeath" at 69. It is brick and has a flat facade, with black shutters and an unadorned doorway. This house was owned by Dr. Robert Kerr, physician to the Indian Department, and rebuilt in 1815 after being burned during the war. Houses of varying sizes obviously lived compatibly side by side in colonial times.

The brick Promenade House stands at 55 Prideaux St., a small hotel of the 1830s which had a dubious reputation. Previously the Niagara Mansion House, it was built in 1819, close to the road and typically shuttered.

Diagonally across Regent Street, on the southeast corner of the intersection, you'll see the brick Stewart House, built around 1830. Its arcaded window treatment, used in Regency buildings, is seen elsewhere in Niagara. The symmetry, shutters, fanlight and sidelights of the period are all present in this house. A grand circular staircase in the entrance hall is a masterpiece of engineering and carpentry.

Continue along Prideaux to No. 18 on the right. This white frame shuttered house, close to the road, belonged to Alexander McKee, a local schoolmaster and was erected in the 1830s. Indoor heating appears to have been effected by stove, as no fireplaces are evident.

Cross the intersection at King Street and follow Picton Street for three blocks to Fort George and Navy Hall. Navy Hall, set on the bank behind Fort George, is *not* open to the public, but was originally a marine storehouse. It is now used for administrative offices. Parks Canada plans to restore it in the future and open it as a museum.

Fort George was built here in the 1790s to oppose the American Fort Niagara. The Americans occupied it in 1813, but it was recaptured by the British after the town was burned in December of that year. Although it survived the War of 1812, it fell into ruins by the mid-1830s. One hundred years later it was reconstructed and is now open to the public, with four daily tours. (Learn more about Fort George in the Museums section of this book.)

From here, you can return to the heart of town for some refreshment or explore farther afield.

St. Andrews' churchyard

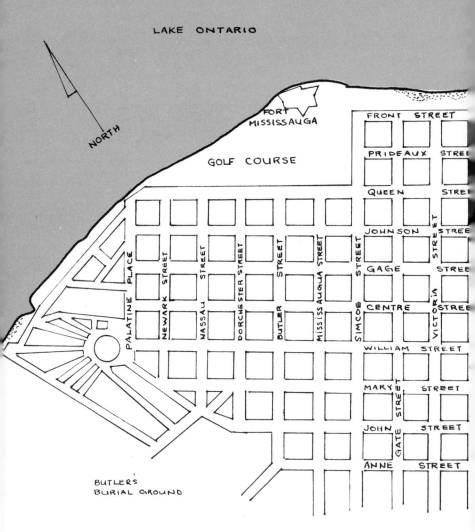

LAKE ONTARIO

NORTH

FORT MISSISSAUGA

GOLF COURSE

FRONT STREET

PRIDEAUX STREE

QUEEN STRE

JOHNSON STREE

GAGE STREE

CENTRE STREE

WILLIAM STREET

MARY STREET

JOHN STREET

ANNE STREET

PALATINE PLACE

NEWARK STREET

NASSAU STREET

DORCHESTER STREET

BUTLER STREET

MISSISSAUGA STREET

SIMCOE STREET

VICTORIA STREET

GATE STREET

BUTLERS
BURIAL GROUND

48

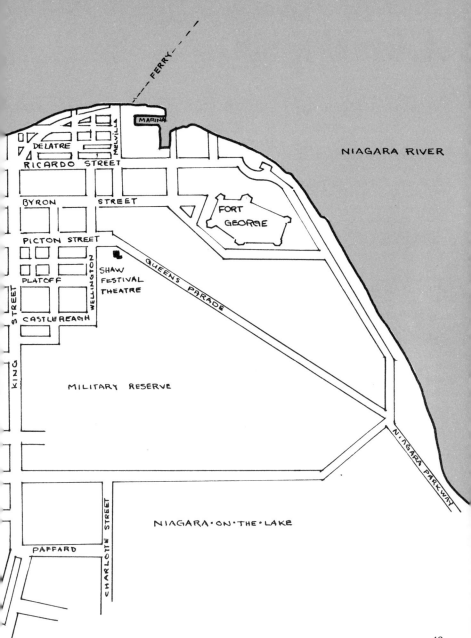

FERRY

NIAGARA RIVER

MARINA

DELATRE

RICARDO STREET

MELVILLE

BYRON STREET

FORT GEORGE

PICTON STREET

PLATOFF

WELLINGTON

SHAW FESTIVAL THEATRE

QUEENS PARADE

CASTLEREAGH

KING STREET

MILITARY RESERVE

NIAGARA PARKWAY

CHARLOTTE STREET

NIAGARA·ON·THE·LAKE

PAFFARD

49

4. Great finds

Whatever you might be looking for — whether it's antiques, health foods, exclusive clothing, or a bookstore — chances are you'll find it on or near Queen Street. Some of the places, we've already mentioned in the downtown walking tour — here they are in more detail. Every store is within a few blocks of each other, which makes shopping temptingly easy. A word of caution: don't assume that shop hours are standard. Niagara's a leisurely sort of place and time is often forgotten.

The Peanut Mill

This is the town's only health food store, just opened in 1976 and featuring peanut butter freshly ground while you watch.

The shelves are stocked with soya beans, rice cakes, granola, lentils, dried fruits, and exotic nuts, and at your feet you'll find bags of whole wheat flour and wheat bran. This is also one of the few health stores with Golden Seal herb in teabags.

There is also a selection of vitamins, non-allergenic cosmetics and popular recipe books for sale.

22 Picton Street (468-7715)
Tuesday to Friday, 10 a.m. to 5:30 p.m. Saturday 10 a.m. to 6 p.m. Summer only, Sundays and holidays, 1 p.m. to 5 p.m. Closed Mondays

The Old Niagara Book Shop

Niagara-on-the-Lake's only bookstore is located in a recently renovated old house with a comfortable homey atmosphere. Laura Trasewick, the owner, has created this warm environment with shelves, gold carpeting, tables covered in pumpkin felt, and rooms lit by brass chandeliers with smoky glass globes. Books are displayed casually and attractively on the tables.

Mrs. Trasewick offers the largest selection of Canadiana and children's books in the Niagara area. You'll find everything from classics to cookbooks and jigsaw puzzles here.

The children's room is comfortably furnished with low tables and chairs and stuffed animals, inviting the young to quietly select their own books.

The historical and artistic bent of the community also demands a wide selection of crafts books, Canadian history, art, gardening, theatre and antiques. Book plates and fashion posters are also kept in stock.

Mrs. Trasewick has justly earned a good reputation for producing quick

Top: The Country Store
Bottom: Joseph's

and dependable results, should the book you need be out of stock.

9 Queen Street (468-2602)
Monday to Saturday, 11 a.m. to 5:30 p.m. Summers only, Sundays 1 p.m. to 5 p.m.

Joseph's & Co.

Once a fire hall, this building has recently undergone a transformation. With the insertion of larger windows and glass display cases, the sun now shines on a glittering display of china, crystal, pewter and brass.

Joseph's long-time reputation for china and gifts of quality makes it a natural stop for gift buying. You'll find such lines as Spode, Ainsley, Minton, Royal Doulton, and Rosenthal, as well as Royal Worcester flameware dishes and Waterford crystal.

Spacious aisles allow plenty of room for browsing among decanters, goblets, silver and brass candelabra, pewter tea sets, and fine porcelain.

10 Queen Street (468-2653)
May 24 to Labor Day, Monday 9 a.m. to 6 p.m. Tuesday to Saturday, 9 a.m. to 8:30 p.m. Sunday 1 p.m. to 8:30 p.m.
Labor Day to May 24, Monday to Saturday, 9 a.m. to 6 p.m. Sunday 12 noon to 6 p.m.
Closed Monday in January, February and March

The Theatre Deli

If you forgot to take the roast out of the freezer before you left home, don't despair — a frozen full-course meal can be yours at The Theatre Deli. Choose from among steak-and-kidney pie, chicken pie, coq au vin, three varieties of quiche, beef stroganoff, duck, Dover sole, lobster or trout, and even tortillas. Just put your selection in the oven and prepare for a treat. Add a salad from the delicatessen cooler, and end with one of the Deli's assorted teas and cheeses.

15 Queen Street (468-2256)
Monday to Thursday, 9 a.m. to 8:30 p.m., Friday and Saturday, 9 a.m. to 10 p.m., Sunday 10 a.m. to 7 p.m.

The Sign of the Pineapple

One of Queen Street's most attractive boutiques, The Sign of the Pineapple dominates the block in a tall, unusually narrow three-storey building of the 1830s. Although it once went through a "depressed stage" as a penny arcade, it has now been painted a cheery yellow and is popular with antique buffs, displaying solid oak hand-carved furniture, rocking chairs, pewter mugs, candlesticks and brassware, sconces and Great Grandson clocks. Available, too, are fireplace fixtures, ceramic figures, silver jewelry by Rafael and J. Michaels, original oils, serigraphs and cookbooks.

The Pineapple's real specialty would appear to be the selection of custom-made brass beds. There are always some on hand, but the majority are ordered from catalogues.

The owners also offer an interior design and mailing service for interested patrons.

16 Queen Street (468-3966)
May 24 to Labor Day, Monday to Friday, 10:30 a.m. to 8:30 p.m., Saturday 10:30 a.m. to 6 p.m., Sunday 10:30 a.m. to 5 p.m.
Labor Day to May 24, Tuesday to Saturday 10:30 a.m. to 5 p.m.

Howe's Antiques

The Country Store
The specialty here is clocks, and you'll find some amazing timepieces in this shop. There are 18-day, spring-wind models, Westminsters chiming every quarter hour — clocks of every shape, size and tone imaginable.

When you've taken in all the timepieces, you might like to turn to the wrought-iron ornaments, wooden sconces, framed mirrors, and lead soldiers from antique molds. Czechoslovakian crystal, place-mats, or scented soaps for the children are also in display.

32 Queen Street (468-3490)
May 24 to Labor Day, Monday to Sunday 11 a.m. to 5:30 p.m.
Labor Day to May 24, Thursday to Sunday 11 a.m. to 5:30 p.m.
July and August, open evenings

Cameron-Jeffries: "The Yardstick"
Both men and women can select from quality sportswear here. Women can choose jewelry and scarves as accessories to soft camel-hair skirts and ultrasuedes, Jaegar woolens and Ports International shirts and dresses. Long summer gowns in bright cottons and jerseys are also ideal for the theatre or evening wear.

Men can select English cardigans and pullovers, sports shirts and imported ties.

46 Queen Street (468-2766)
April to October only, Monday to Saturday, 9 a.m. to 5 p.m.

Greaves' Jams and Jellies
In 1928 William Greaves began producing marmalades, jams and jellies on his farm outside of town.

As his trade flourished, he moved his retail outlet into this century-old building on Queen Street, once a grocery store. The Greaves business continues here today, its delightful aromas wafting from the rear of the store where vats bubble with berries, peaches, grapes, and citrus fruits.

You'll find every variety of berry jam, cherry, grape, citrus, and combinations sold here, as well as combinations such as apricot-almond marmalade, peach jam, and chili sauce — gift wrapped, if you wish. There are also gift boxes of three or six small jars of different combinations from $3.50 up.

55 Queen Street (468-7831)
Monday to Saturday, 9 a.m. to 6 p.m.

Howe's Antiques
Behind the blue-and-white-checkered curtains gleam treasures in brass and copper, chunky Canadian goblets, fine old china, curios and a special assortment of excellent Primitive pieces in furniture. Marguerita Howe's specialty is early Canadian furniture and utensils, so look for unique old wood-framed mirrors, candlesticks, lamps, and prints.

61 Queen Street (468-3328)
Labor Day to May 24, Monday to Sunday, 12:30 p.m. to 5:30 p.m.
May 24 to Labor Day, evenings as well. Call first, hours are flexible.

McCrae Hall
This charming little shop is housed in the first telegraph office in Upper Canada, purchased by the McCraes and restored in 1966.

The shop is appealingly cluttered with what Mrs. McCrae describes as "her treasures." And treasures there are. You could spend hours going through the amazing variety of soaps, jellies, antiques and jewelry. The delicate strains of "Bless This House", played on a music box attached to the door, will greet you.

Of special interest to collectors at the time this was written were the original snuff boxes, a Percheron stallion (one of 500 modelled by Doris Lindner), the Mayflower bowl produced by Royal Worcester to commemorate the 350th anniversary of the sailing of the Pilgrim Fathers, and a "loving mug" issued by Spode China for Queen Elizabeth and Prince Philip's 25th wedding anniversary.

Look for the plump "Suttles and Seawinds" comforters. For another kind of luxury, pick up a box of Gourmet Truffles and Godiva Chocolates (the world's finest), recent additions to the store's treasures.

At the back of the store is a tearoom where you can enjoy an afternoon tea of garnished sandwiches, walnut coffee cake, tortes, colonial cookies and other treats on the menu. Summertime may find you enjoying brunch at a small table in the rose garden behind the shop.

65 Queen Street (468-7187)
Daily 10 a.m. to 6 p.m., tearoom, 10 a.m. to 5:30 p.m.
Closed only on Christmas Day and Boxing Day

The Niagara Home Bakery
The town's only bakery; it's family-owned and well-known for its baked goods and imaginative holiday displays.

Every season or special occasion calls for a festive window decoration, designed to lure customers with a sweet tooth inside. The aroma of fresh-baked bread does the rest! Once inside, you'll be faced with the temptations of butter tarts, raisin cookies, donuts, and hermit cookies.

In autumn, pumpkins and gourds are gaily piled among cakes and appropriately decorated in Halloween orange, while black paper witches swing around gingerbread men.

At Christmas, the bakery resembles

McClelland's Store today   *and yesterday...*

a child's vision of Santa's workshop. Holly, mistletoe, a gingerbread house, reindeer cookies, and special holiday cakes will weaken the stoniest Scrooge.

66 Queen Street (468-3431)
Tuesday to Saturday, 9 a.m. to 5:45 p.m.

McClelland's West End Store

When you enter McClelland's your eyes and nose will carry you quickly back to the 1790s. The first thing you'll probably notice is the sloping wooden floor. The lingering scent of spices, teas and cheese reinforces the rarefied atmosphere of the pioneer merchant, and it is easy to visualize the early townspeople seated cozily near the original roaring fireplace (which is now covered), conversing with neighbors and sipping liquor offered by the white-aproned grocer.

McClelland's has records of tran-

sactions from the 1880s and accounts which ran for several generations. Once they sold such exotic items as Orris Root and Musk Oil, teas and spices from around the world, lamp oil, cigars and "galloons," or laces threaded with gold and silver.

Today, McClelland's is famous for its cheeses, purchased in 90 lb. cases and allowed to age before being sold. At the back of the store you may sample and choose from among 40 to 50 varieties of cheese. A tempting gourmet section displays pickled walnuts, scallop soup, mushroom ketchup, rum cakes, chestnut purée, patés, pickled mushrooms and corn, English biscuits and crackers, and smoked oysters. This is a must-stop for food-and-nostalgia lovers.

106 Queen Street (468-7639)
Monday to Saturday, 9 a.m. to 6 p.m., Friday 9 a.m. to 9 p.m.

Viking Antiques

If you are a collector of Christmas plates, you'll find a good selection at the Viking — Kaiser, Hummel, Royal Copenhagen, Wedgwood, and Bing Grondhal are all featured here. And owner Kurt Sorensen offers a vast mail order service for his collector-customers.

Primarily a curio shop, Viking is a good place to look for copper and brassware, small pieces of furniture, butter bowls, pressed glass, and candle snuffers. You'll also find an ample assortment of reproductions in horse brasses.

122 Queen Street (telephone Hurley's Flower Shop, 468-3129)
May 24 to Labor Day, Monday to Sunday, 1 p.m. to 5 p.m.
Labor Day to May 24, weekends only, 1 p.m. to 5 p.m.

Arnold's Antiques

For 30 years owner W.G. Helwig has been collecting some of the finest Canadian and English antique furniture in the area. Now he spends much of his time refinishing these pieces for sale in his shop.

In the rear of the store is a small gallery of prints and samples of picture frames, both antique and modern. If you climb up the stairs to the loft, you might be able to find a schoolmaster's desk, a Windsor chair, a tilt-top table, or a rare Deacon's bench.

135 Queen Street (468-3651)
April to December, Monday to Saturday, 9:30 a.m. to 5 p.m., Sunday 1 p.m. to 5 p.m.
Closed January through March

Country Togs, Part I and Part II

Don Driedger and Bill Greaves opened these shops in 1975 to offer up-to-date fashions for Niagara's country gentleman. Part I outfits younger men in denims of all kinds — jackets, shirts and trousers. Part II carries more conservative wear, from suits and dress shirts to suede jackets.

34 Queen Street (468-7545)
May 24 to Labor Day, Monday to Friday, 10 a.m. to 9 p.m., Saturday, 10 a.m. to 6 p.m., Sunday 1 p.m. to 5 p.m.
Labor Day to May 24, closed evenings and Sundays

Ted Ball's Fish Shop

Ted Ball earns his living fishing at the mouth of the Niagara River. Following in the footsteps of his father, uncle and grandfather, he catches salmon, white bass, perch, pickerel, and smelts, and sells them at dockside in the Spring and Fall.

From April to June, and September to November, he sets out with his dog at dusk to place his nets along the shoreline. By dawn, his homemade green fiberglass boat, Cucumber II can be seen drifting along on the horizon.

If his sign reads "Fish," you can find Ted cleaning and selling his catch in his shop. In the Fall, you can also buy smoked salmon cured on the premises.

87 River Beach (468-3338)
Spring and Fall only. (Look for the silver float, and the fishnet drying in the sun.)

Ted Ball on Cucumber II

5. Arts and crafts

Niagara-on-the-Lake is especially appealing for its wide selection of arts and crafts offerings. Here you can find handicrafts of every description — from wood carvings and leatherware to stuffed animals and ponchos. Some are made by local craftsmen; others are imported from as far away as Ireland and Scotland. Niagara-on-the-Lake even has its own needlework centre for those who want to create their own patterns.

The Owl and the Pussycat

Just a half block from The Shaw Festival Theatre, there's a small colonial shop with pine fixtures and antique lamps. Here in quaint, bright surroundings you'll find handrubbed pine furniture, antique and bisque dolls, children's wooden toys and stuffed animals. Owner Regina Prugh makes the Gretchen fabric dolls herself.

Moffat Mews, 60 Picton Street (468-3081)
Wednesday to Sunday, 1 p.m. to 5 p.m.
Closed Monday and Tuesday
Summer hours somewhat longer to accommodate theatregoers

The Doll Shop

If you have a doll-lover in your family, don't miss this boutique. The Doll Shop was started by three young people as an outlet for handmade dolls crafted by local women, and the variety is amazing. Imagine an "inchworm who has eaten his dinner," or an octopus doll; look for upside-down dolls with double personalities. Also on hand are crocheted clothes for Barbie dolls, Teddy bears with fireproof stuffing, Raggedy-Ann and Andy, and patchwork dolls.

23 Queen Street (enter through Warren Heating & Plumbing) (468-2127)
End of May to September, Monday to Sunday, 9 a.m. to 5 p.m.
Evenings on weekends

The Cobblestone Gallery

This small, well-known gallery on Mary Street has recently moved half a block for the sake of expansion, and plans for the new larger gallery include rooms full of art, watercolors, prints, pottery and sculpture.

Presently, Pat Fanstone, the dynamic curator, is offering paintings of quality by Canadian artists and in addition to selling their work, holds "Meet the Artist" exhibits for art lovers who enjoy her lively, informative talks.

Among those whose works can be

Top: The Doll Shop
Bottom: The Cobblestone Gallery

purchased here are James Kierstead, Conrad Von Suchtelen, Campbell Scott and Ken Hanson.

A framing service is also available here.

463 King Street (468-2097)
May 24 to Labor Day, Wednesday to Sunday, 11 a.m. to 6 p.m. Evenings by appointment.
Labor Day to May 24, weekends and by appointment

The Pillar and Post: Arts and Handcraft Shoppe

Open the door to the left of The Pillar and Post entrance for an excursion into Canadiana. The Inn's show-rooms are packed with crafts, gift items, decorating pieces and pine furniture.

Giant Raggedy-Ann dolls rest on a pile of patchwork pillows in a pine rocking chair, while a doll's crib nearby is laden with beautiful quilts. Crisp pinafores and aprons hang in a wardrobe along a wall, and small round tables are hidden beneath a wealth of trinkets, pottery, woven placemats, notepaper, soap, patchwork flowerpots and oven mitts. The walls abound with paintings, prints, hangings and samplers, appropriately Canadiana. The selection of calicos and printed cottons here is the largest in the peninsula.

Authentic reproductions of pine furniture are always available, and wrought iron fixtures and sculptures are made to order in the inn's forge.

John Street at King (468-2123)
Daily from 10 a.m. to 9 p.m.

The Nimble Needle

If you've joined the legions of those recently addicted to "needling" you might want to get in touch with Betty Mitchell.

Betty offers a popular selection of courses for beginners and advanced students in the fine art of needle and canvas. It's by appointment only, but aficianados of this art won't want to miss her classes. Betty is a member of the Embroiderers' Guild of America and much of her work is displayed in her studio. Supplies are also available here: Paternayan Persian yarns, Mono canvases of varying gauges, and custom designs, as well as some of the fun kits for tennis racquet covers, belts and evening bags, Christmas stockings and decorations.

This is not strictly a female past-time; men are becoming equally enthusiastic about "needling" for relaxation. Betty welcomes men and women, and she even has a few small pieces for interested children to start on.

The cost varies according to the size of the canvas and amount of wool needed. Some small pieces, such as coasters and key rings, start at $3.75.

Beginner Course — a sampler of students' own house, including canvas, wool and instruction, is $33 for four weeks.

Advanced Course — such as shading, and more complicated stitchery, is $35.

217 Butler Street (468-3120)
By appointment only

The Celtic Shop

Here is a combination shop-and-gallery offering crafts and batiks on display and for sale. The small shop, divided into three areas, carries batiks and dolls, assorted pottery, jewelry, and gift items, and a needlepoint and knitting section.

You'll find rings, pins, and fancy beaded sandals at the jewelry counter. Then look over the Mohawk pottery, pebble people, sculptures of metal and stone, and stuffed animals especially handmade for the shop. You might even be tempted to buy a bird feeder with a squirrel guard for your backyard.

The Irish batiks for sale in the gallery are the work of artisan Norah Golden.

40 Queen Street (468-2642)
Monday to Wednesday and Saturday, 10 a.m. to 5:30 p.m., Thursday and Friday, 10 a.m. to 9 p.m., Sunday noon to 5:30 p.m.

Exclusive Leather
If you're looking for unique leather clothing or accessories, visit Gary Jenney. He'll create anything from leather seats for your Corvette to hot pants, and can show you samples of leather bags, belts, sandals. He also repairs luggage, purses and anything in leather. Among Gary's credits are his design of the leggings, girths and thong sandals for such Shaw productions as *Caesar and Cleopatra.*

212 Regent Street, just behind 46 Queen (468-3130)
Labor Day to May 24, Monday to Sunday, 9 a.m. to 9 p.m.
May 24 to Labor Day, closed Sunday

Schmidt's Arts and Handicrafts
Niagara-on-the-Lake's French heritage comes to life in this spacious shop, featuring hand-woven wall hangings, vests, ponchos, handbags, skirts and neckties, Quebec woodcarvings, and ceramic chess sets.

Scotland and Iceland are also represented by long woolen skirts and capes, and chunky, warm Nordic sweaters.

St. David's pottery by Desmond Shephard, lead glass hangings and lamps make a colorful display and are also for sale.

Prices may seem steep but merchandise is of the highest quality and design.

59 Queen Street (468-3303)
Summer, Monday to Saturday, 10 a.m. to noon, 1 p.m. to 6 p.m. Closed Sunday
October to April, Tuesday to Friday, 1 p.m. to 5 p.m., Saturday, 10 a.m. to noon, 1 p.m. to 5 p.m. Closed Sunday

The Gingham Patch
This shop is full of surprises, beginning with its size. The small-paned window gives it a dollhouse look from the outside, but the inside is spacious and holds a wealth of treasures for children and adults.

There are plastic place mats and washable crayon sets to keep toddlers occupied at the table between courses, and upside-down dolls, scrabble sentence games and scribblers for children, too.

Proprietor Bob Koehler makes furniture to order, if you have a special piece in mind, or you can select from among his Canadian reproductions in the shop, including pine headboards, dry sinks, hutches, and shelves.

Regent Street at Queen (468-2792)
Tuesday to Sunday, noon to 5 p.m.

6. Museums, churches and memorabilia

Niagara-on-the-Lake is a contemporary cameo of the 1800s — a time in history which continues to intrigue us today. The Niagara Historical Museum features Indian artifacts, Laura Secord's kettle and General Brock's hat, bringing yesterday to life, and nearby forts and museums reflect life in an era of violent war. The churches in contrast, highlight the Niagarans' inward struggle to find peace.

FORT GEORGE

Fort George is one of Canada's few forts whose authenticity has been maintained. The original fort was built in 1796 to replace Fort Niagara which the British were forced to relinquish by treaty that year to the Americans. Although poorly located strategically, far from the river mouth and on the outskirts of the town, the fort was primarily intended to temporarily house the British regiments inside its palisade. The plan was to build small earth bastions for cannon, create a lookout, and include a powder magazine with cedar picketing, and a shallow dry ditch. Because Governor Simcoe recognized the inadequacy of this as a defense for Newark, he moved the Capital away, but Fort George remained as the only garrison.

Three years before the War of 1812, General Brock was assigned to this fort, and was later given a military burial amidst a booming gun salute from both sides of the river.

Later in the war, in May 1813, Fort George was bombarded for two days and suffered heavy casualties. Cannon fire from Fort Niagara and the enemy fleet in the river were continued threats. When the log buildings and stockade were demolished by cannon fire, the regiments withdrew to a safer position. American troops took over the fort and remained there for seven months, making some repairs to the ruined fortification while stationed there and strengthening its fortifications.

The British, with the help of their Indian friends, managed to defeat the enemy in battle in Canadian bush nearby and bottled up the Americans at Fort George. Then began a long, patient wait until winter. By this time, many of the entrapped American troops had wandered from the fort, often deserting because of cold weather, sickness or sheer boredom. Realizing their predicament, the American commanding officer, General McClure, ordered a retreat across the river. As a parting gesture of revenge,

Fort George, built in 1796

Fort George kitchen display

the town of Newark was set to the torch.

That same month, the British, again ensconced in the heavily damaged Fort George, crossed the river and seized Fort Niagara. The area surrounding it was scorched, as well as Buffalo, and while in possession of the American fort, the British began constructing a more permanent Canadian fort, Fort Mississauga. Fort George continued to serve as a depot and small barracks until it fell into utter decay and was finally abandoned in 1826. In the 1930s, the provincial and federal governments agreed to rebuild the barracks, including the officers' quarters, mess halls, the guardhouse, blacksmith shop, and kitchen as it had existed in the early 1800s. Although fully restored by 1940, the official opening was postponed until after the Second World War, and both Canadian and Ameri-

can military personnel attended the special ceremony in June 1950. In 1969 the Federal Department of Indian and Northern Affairs declared the site a National Park, and began further renovations.

Entering the palisade, you'll see neat log buildings with the British Union Jack of King George III flying proudly above. Go inside the barracks to stretch out on the wooden bunks arranged in precise rows, the ones closest to the large open fireplace doubtless belonging to soldiers of superior rank.

In one of the barracks you'll see a display of tools and equipment used by men who obviously required strength and endurance. Muskets, bugles, cannonballs, warming pans, ice skates and spinning wheels testify to a rigorous existence. The blacksmith shop stands today, anvil waiting, as though the craftsmen had just stepped out. The officers' quarters also await the return of weary men, red coats thrown over the four poster beds, wine carafes and fruit resting on writing tables, tri-cornered hat boxes, muskets and a sleeping cat on a rocking chair.

In the open kitchen behind the barracks, you'll find a lifelike display of bread in the making, fish ready for frying, cheese, fruit and vegetables to be prepared for hearty appetites.

Why not try out the stocks and the jail cells, next on your tour?

A log cabin outside the fort's palisade serves as the ticket office, and sells souvenirs, brochures and refreshments. Admission: adults $1, family $3.50, students 50¢, school groups $2, senior citizens and children under 4, free.

Niagara River Parkway (468-2741) May 15 to September 15, daily 9 a.m. to 6 p.m. Tours at 9 a.m., 10:30 a.m., 1 p.m., 2:30 p.m.

NAVY HALL

Just below the present Fort George on the river bank is an oblong grey stone building, the sole remainder of four provincial marine storehouses for naval equipment. Here, ships coming from Kingston picked up supplies and made repairs. These buildings were erected in 1797.

When Governor Simcoe arrived in the colony, one of the storehouses was converted into living quarters to accommodate himself and his wife. This was doubtless a change for an aristocratic Englishman and his lady, but they were probably compensated by the magnificent view of the river from their window. And in these quarters, Simcoe was to assemble the first Parliament of Upper Canada in 1792.

Navy Hall was first restored by the Dominion Government in 1912. The building was originally a frame one that was later encased in stone. Eventually the hall will become a museum, with exhibits demonstrating its history of the naval defence of Lake Ontario. At present, it is not open to the public, but it is visible from the Niagara River Parkway.

FORT MISSISSAUGA

This neglected old fort is one of few star-shaped forts in North America, constructed of rubble carried by farmers' wagons after the razing of the town. It was erected on this site in 1814 because of its location directly opposite Fort Niagara across the river. (Residents felt Fort George should have been built here for better access to the river and observation of the enemy fort.) Originally surrounded by eight log buildings used as barracks, the tower stored powder and cannon. But in 1815 the Treaty of Ghent forestalled its operation and never a shot was fired. Soldiers continued on duty here until 1840.

The fort is now inaccessible, standing lonely vigil at the tip of the golf course, fenced off by the Federal Government to protect it from vandalism until restoration takes place.

Plans are to open the fort to the public in 1981, after its restoration by Parks Canada to its original appearance. The 48 acres surrounding the fort, now a golf course, will become a

Old Fort Mississauga, built in 1814. From an old postcard

recreational area.

On Mississauga Point by the Lake

THE NIAGARA HISTORICAL SOCIETY MUSEUM

Nestled behind a white picket fence, inside a small brick courtyard is the oldest museum in Upper Canada.

In 1895, Janet Carnochan, principal of the local high school and a staunch United Empire Loyalist, founded the Historical Society. Twelve years later she supervised the building of Memorial Hall next door to her school, as a site to display the artifacts and memorabilia of colonial days. In 1972, the Historical Society joined together both the school and Memorial Hall to enlarge their quarters.

Inside you'll find General Brock's hat, resplendent with white ostrich plumes, red and white cockade and gold plated chain. Alas, it was never worn, as it arrived from England after the General was killed in battle. Also in display are hackles owned by Butler's Rangers, many of Laura Secord's personal possessions, porcelain dolls, cradles, spinning wheels,

and iron cooking pots hanging in the ktichen fireplace. Upstairs in the gallery is a dugout canoe, a sausage stuffer dating back to 1890, and antique prints and primitive oils.

Colorful Redcoat uniforms of the War of 1812, ladies' dainty fans and bonnets, and tiny-waisted silk dresses are all carefully preserved for viewing. There are many Indian relics on display as well.

The Museum is now actively involved in community activities on a year round basis. Once a month there are films, lectures, displays and demonstrations. Walking and bus tours for adults are arranged here, and children from Quebec and Ontario schools enjoy conducted educational tours. At Christmas time, the Historical Society Carollers bring pleasure to the townspeople. Other activities welcoming public participation are the Simcoe Ball every other year in June, the Simcoe Tea held in the courtyard in the summer with the "Governor and his Lady" in costume, an annual Levée in June to commemorate the birthday of King George III, and a fall garden party in one of the historic homes. The dates change, so consult the Museum for specific information.

In spring, the Museum offers a Kettledrum, an eighteenth century cocktail party originally held for regimental officers and their ladies, where you'll enter an elegant era of velvet coats, satin gowns and the stately quadrilles of the "Simcoe Dancers." Guests are announced with a roll of the drums and the banquet table provides a bountiful variety of canapés in keeping with those served in the 1800s.

The Society is currently preparing a cookbook of eighteenth century recipes and sells herbs in the summer from a herb garden at the rear of the Museum.

For a guided tour of Niagara-on-the-Lake, or a group visit to the Museum, write to the Society at the following address, or phone ahead.

Admission: adults $1, children 50¢.

43 Castlereagh Street (468-3912)
May 15 to September 15, 1 p.m. to 7 p.m.
Winter, Wednesday, Saturday, Sunday 1 p.m. to 5 p.m.

THE COURT HOUSE

Built in 1847, this was the last official building created while Niagara-on-the-Lake still housed government bodies and legislators. Although the Governor General and most departments had gone, there were still some branches remaining in town. It was hoped that the government branches would linger in the impressive, three-storied building erected on the site of Government House before the War of 1812.

In recent years the Court House has been converted into a theatre named for it, and other spacious rooms are used for civic functions. Because the cost of repairing and restoring this classic structure has become so expensive, it can no longer be financed by public funds. A Citizens' Committee is now preparing to raise money privately for its renovation.

12 Queen Street (no phone)
Monday to Saturday, 9 a.m. to 5 p.m.
Summer, open evenings for the theatre.

NIAGARA-ON-THE-LAKE PUBLIC LIBRARY

Niagara's first library service was formed in 1800, and within a year 80 books were collected, mostly religious and non-fiction works. By 1812, there were 827 volumes, but these were destroyed or stolen by retreating American soldiers.

After the war, as more volumes accumulated, two rooms were set aside in the Court House for the library. Brock University in St. Catharines now stores all the historical documents and catalogues pertaining to Niagara-on-the-Lake.

The entrance to the library with its ornate Georgian doorway with pilasters, fanlight and panelled door in keeping with the building's architecture, was restored in 1974. Gas light standards were originally planned but never installed.

Today, along with regular library services, the library offers children's films and numerous educational programs.

St. Mark's Church

26 Queen Street, rear of the Court
House (468-2023)
Tuesday to Friday, 1 p.m. to 9 p.m.,
Saturday 9 a.m. to 5 p.m., Sunday 2
p.m. to 5 p.m.
Closed Monday in winter; Sunday
and Monday in summer

THE NIAGARA APOTHECARY

Today's medicines might be more efficient, but they surely lack the glamor of some of the more exotic remedies available when the Apothecary opened its doors on this site in 1866.

Whatever happened to "Kickapoo Indian Sagwa" for a long life and "Egyptian Regulation Tea" for indigestion, constipation, dyspepsia, consumption, blood disease, nervous disability, corpulency, liver complaint, kidney disease and sick headaches?

Licorice root, cascara bark, fig pills for the liver, and leeches for high blood pressure and black eyes were a lot more colorful than aspirin, acromycin and trulfacillin.

This is the oldest pharmacy in Upper Canada, opened by Henry Pafford, a licensed pharmacist and once Mayor of the town, whose "Golden Mortar" still hangs over the door. As a licensed chemist, he also displayed the two show globes still in the window, formerly lit by a candle.

When the last pharmacist closed the store in 1964, the Niagara Foundation purchased the building to preserve it. The Ontario College of Pharmacy and the Ontario Heritage Foundation received two awards for the excellence and authenticity shown in restoring the Apothecary.

Take a look at the ornate black walnut counters, inscribed cabinets and drawers and three crystal chandeliers, exact reproductions of the originals. The 100-year-old cash register is the second machine made by the National Cash Register Co., and still has the original paper, a combination lock, inkwell and feather pen.

Sundays, on their way to church, the ladies of the day dropped in to use the metal perfume dispenser. By inserting a penny and pulling a handle, they could be sprayed with scent. If you'd like to use this apparatus today, inflation requires that you insert a quarter.

Children will be fascinated by medicine bottles shaped like fish, pigs and people; worm killer salves and medicine spoons with trap doors. There's nothing for sale here — it's strictly a museum.

No admission charge.

5 Queen Street (468-7312)
May to September, noon to 6:30 p.m.
Closed in winter

THE FIRE HALL MUSEUM

After 1813, fire left an indelible scar on Niagara-on-the-Lake. Small wonder then, that the town maintains a fire company museum, complete with its primitive equipment. Wooden water wagons and buckets were hoisted and hauled by hand, while hoses and reels were dragged over pebbled roads in a desperate attempt to save the frame dwellings. An antique pumper of gleaming red and brass stands in this tiny one room museum surrounded by black fire hats, horns, axes and station insignia.

The exhibit is operated by the Niagara-on-the-Lake volunteer fire department. Donations to the maintenance of this project are gratefully accepted.

Free admission.

King Street near Queen (no phone)
Summer only, Tuesday to Saturday 1 p.m. to 8 p.m.

ST. MARK'S ANGLICAN CHURCH

The Reverend Dr. Addison, a Church of England missionary arriving in Newark in 1792, records that a congregation was formed that year. There was no place for them to worship, however, so in 1804 church members erected a rectangular stone building resembling an English parish church. Its adjoining churchyard served as one of the first burial grounds in Upper Canada, and gravestones of the town's earliest settlers can be found here.

During the War of 1812, British forces used the church's solid protection as a hospital for the wounded and for storage. In 1813 the building was partially gutted by fire but its stone walls remained standing and Americans used it as a barracks.

The church was rebuilt in "Cruciform" style in 1843, featuring two high pulpits, Gothic in design, a stained glass east window, galleries and box pews.

In 1892 benches replaced the box pews, galleries were removed and the organ moved to the chancel. Eventual-ly stained glass windows replaced clear ones, with the oldest being installed in 1843.

In recent years the organ and choir have been relocated in the gallery, a font with cover designed and executed by local sculptress Jacobine Jones, and a superb window by Yvonne Williams added.

41 Byron Street (468-3123)
Sunday services at 9 a.m. and 11 a.m.

ST. MARK'S RECTORY

Beside the Church Hall stands a handsome yellow brick Anglican Rectory built in 1858, designed like a Tuscan villa with a square tower and wide bracketed eaves. The fireplaces are on the inside walls and are built out into the rooms, with their chimneys panelled in the square trim of the Tuscan style. Sweeping up from the entrance hall, a magnificent spiral staircase of oak ascends to the tower rooms.

The Rector of St. Mark's lives here today, and the building is not open to the public.

ST. ANDREW'S PRESBYTERIAN CHURCH

In 1794, a group of Presbyterians gathered to discuss construction of a meeting house on land granted by the Crown. The same year, a building in Greek Doric style was designed by, and executed by, a man named Cooper, a craftsman of the highest quality.

In 1813 St. Andrew's was destroyed by fire, but by 1831 it had been totally reconstructed, including its graceful Grecian columns, roundheaded windows and dignified steeple.

The simple but striking interior is decorated in the Classical Renaissance tradition. A gallery supported by slender columns rises above the box pews, painted white and cushioned in red. The oddly-placed pulpit is at the front of the church between its two entrances, with its pulpitum detailed in rich black walnut.

The churchyard may be of interest to those curious about the town's ancestry.

Simcoe Street (no phone)
Sunday services at 11 a.m.

THE MANSE

At the corner of Simcoe and Centre Streets stands the classically Georgian Manse, or Pastor's home, constructed in 1836 by the minister, Dr. Robert McGill. Obviously a man of strong sympathies, McGill housed runaway slaves in the basement during the 1830s.

The house is hip roofed with a centre door and fanlight. In 1975, the original pink brick and cut stone were restored, and many of the fireplaces repaired inside, along with their carved mantels. The minister's study today is the same room used by Dr. McGill, and the pine floors are unretouched.

ST. VINCENT DE PAUL CHURCH

This was the first Roman Catholic church to be erected in the Niagara Peninsula. In 1834, on land granted them beside today's Simcoe Park, the Papists built their church of timber and clapboard in the attractive Gothic

Revival style, with long, vertical pointed windows, and a vaulted ceiling supported by Doric columns with Ionic caps.

In 1965, with the growth of the parish, it became necessary to enlarge the church, and the late Mr. R.O. Petman, a parishioner, provided the funds as a memorial to his first wife on the stipulation that the original interior be preserved. The wooden ceiling of groined vaulting is the original, dating from 1834.

73 Picton Street (468-7272)
Saturday Mass, 7 p.m., Sunday Mass, 9 a.m. and 11 a.m.

MCFARLAND HOUSE

John McFarland, "His Majesty's Boatbuilder," was a Scottish Loyalist who served George III and was a close friend of General Isaac Brock. He was granted Crown land along the Niagara River about one mile south of Fort George, and in 1800 built his home here. It was a handsome structure of handmade brick, which today exemplifies the early Georgian architecture adopted by pioneer settlers.

McFarland was taken prisoner by the invading American army in May, 1813, some months after his friend Brock was killed in battle. His house was converted to a hospital for both British and American soldiers, depending upon who held the land at the time. When the retreating armies set Newark afire in December, 1813,

St. Andrews' Church, 1912

McFarland's house was ransacked and partially burned.

John McFarland died shortly after his return from prison, and his son James rebuilt and occupied the house some years later. A wing on the river side was added in 1892, and the front door was moved to its present location.

The Niagara Parks Commission acquired the McFarland property in 1943 and authentically restored the house, establishing picnic areas on the ample grounds, and opening to sightseers the river bank where the British hid their boats from the enemy in 1813. A picnic pavillion with fireplaces for barbecues is available to the public, as well as a snack bar in the back wing of the house.

Inside the house, the parlor, dining room and bedroom have been furnished in the Loyalist tradition with acid-etched crystal chandeliers, ornate settees, a spinet and four-poster beds. Although not open to the public, the original kitchen is located in the basement where three large bake ovens are housed in solid stone walls.

Admission: Adults 50¢, children under 12, free.

Niagara River Parkway (468-3322)
Wednesdays to Sunday from Victoria Day to Labor Day
Closed Monday and Tuesday

FIELD HOUSE

The Field House, was built the same year of similar red brick construction, and stands a couple of miles away, near Service Road 60 on the Parkway. Built by Gilbert Field, a member of Butler's Rangers, it was rented by

Butler's Burying Ground, early 1900s

General Brock in 1812 as a barracks. It suffered damage by cannonfire from the American shore but was restored by Col. Robert Cudney and the Ontario Heritage Foundation. The public may visit it during the Annual House Tour.

BUTLER'S BARRACKS

John Butler was an American pioneer and Loyalist soldier who led a small band of loyal Britons during the American Revolution. Using "guerilla warfare," Butler's Rangers, with Indian help, attacked, plundered and destroyed American settlements where rebels congregated, thereby preventing rebel armies from seizing control of the Great Lakes basin. Overcrowded in their base at Fort Niagara on the American side, Colon-

el Butler brought his company to the west bank to construct their own barracks in 1778. The building, of huge hand-cut pine timbers, was held together with pegs.

The Rangers passed the winters here until 1784 when they disbanded, many settling with their families in the area as private citizens on lands granted by the Crown to which they had remained so steadfast.

The Barracks were put to military use again in the War of 1812, the Fenian raids of 1866, and during World Wars I and II.

When the site was about to be demolished some years ago, local historians opposed the move and the Federal Government temporarily protected the landmark with corrugated iron sheathing. Restoration plans are now under way by the Ontario Heritage Foundation for a monument to the loyalty of the "buckskin warriors."

King Street at Mary
Not yet open to public

BUTLER'S BURYING GROUND

Butler Street leads to a quiet burying ground on a grassy knoll, where the bodies of Colonel John Butler and his family are laid to rest on his land. The gravesite has been carefully maintained by the Niagara Parks Commission since 1912, with the gravestones cemented in neat, slanting rows, and carefully repaired or authentically replaced, if irreparable.

Colonel Butler's grave is unmarked, but you'll notice a plaque and a stone monument on the grounds.

7. Theatres great and small

For many, the chief attraction of Niagara-on-the-Lake is its excellent selection of theatre. There's mime at the Royal George and Shaw at the Shaw Festival Theatre. But there's even more ...

THE SHAW FESTIVAL THEATRE

The Shaw Festival was conceived in 1961 by Brian Doherty, a local lawyer. During a discussion of ways to stimulate public interest in Niagara-on-the-Lake, he hit upon the idea of a theatre. The works of Bernard Shaw were selected, both because of their sophistication and suitability as "festival" material. Within days, committees and volunteers were set up and Doherty, who was an old hand at organizing theatre groups, began the search for money, actors and a stage.

That summer, the first performance, *Don Juan in Hell,* was produced at the old Court House Theatre — appropriately, in the middle of a heat wave! Henceforth, the Theatre has immortalized Shaw with a growing number of fine actors, including Kate Reid, Barry Morse, Paxton Whitehead, Zoe Caldwell and Stanley Holloway. The Queen and Prince Philip, Prime Minister Pierre Trudeau, and Madame Indira Ghandi are among those notables who have attended performances here. The story behind Doherty's tremendously successful venture is documented in his book, *Not Bloody Likely.*

In 1971, award-winning architect Ron Thom designed a new brick theatre in which to hold performances of Shaw's works. Low in profile, dramatically graceful, it complements the historic town; its striking interior houses 822 seats, selected works of art, a handwoven theatre curtain and a library. Glass walls in the main lobby and balconies offer magnificent views of terraces, a reflecting pool, green fields, and scenic Queen's Parade Road.

"Shaw" has initiated a number of other activities to further the arts. In winter, concerts featuring artists such as the Canadian Opera Company, the Royal Winnipeg Ballet, and the King Singers from England, are well-attended. Senior citizens can enjoy a film program on winter Wednesday afternoons at 2 p.m. Between October and March, enthusiastic groups from

Three major Shaw Festival figures: Top is Brian Doherty who conceived the idea of a festival for Niagara; bottom left, "Cleopatra" and right, George Bernard Shaw himself.

all over the peninsula arrive by bus to enjoy such films as *The Red Shoes, Treasure Island,* the *Great Waltz,* and *Lawrence of Arabia.* Cost is 75¢ for senior citizens, $1.50 for the general public. A coffee hour follows each show. Summer residencies for concert artists offer a performing stage for the artist, and give students an opportunity to benefit from working with the guest in residence.

Seminars on Shaw organized by the Festival and the School of Adult Education at McMaster University are also a popular summer supplement to the theatre. Given concurrently with Shaw's plays, they provide an in-depth study of the playwright, his techniques, and philosophies. Lecturers from Canadian, British and American universities have offered their views on such topics as Shaw and Ibsen, Shaw and the Great Composers, and Shaw and 19th Century Theatre.

A privately run ballet school held in the rehearsal hall is attended by enthusiastic children and adults all year round.

With the success of these activities, future plans are afoot for winter residencies of opera companies, dance groups, voice classes, and experimental theatre.

For information regarding any of the above activities, call or write to the Theatre. Tickets for performances

Intermission in the Festival Theatre's pleasant court yard

range from $5 to $10. An annual membership of $25 offers select tickets before they are sold through the box office, as well as advance mailings for all coming events.

Wellington Street and Queen's Parade Road (468-3201)
Toronto Box Office (361-1544)
Open all year
Matinees: Wednesday and Sunday, 5 p.m., Saturday, 2:30 p.m.
Evenings: Tuesday to Saturday, 8:30 p.m.

THE OLD COURT HOUSE THEATRE

While George Bernard Shaw is being celebrated at the new Shaw Festival Theatre, the old Court House simultaneously hosts a series of Shaw-related productions. Plays by Shaw contemporaries such as Ibsen, Ben Travers, and William Goldring reflect their times, and alternate with rollicking French period bedroom farces. This small, intimate theatre is in a meeting room converted into an informal stage, where the close involvement with the audience is strikingly different in atmosphere from the massive Festival Theatre.

Information and tickets can be obtained from the Shaw Festival Box Office (below). Tickets range from $5 to $7.

12 Queen Street (468-3201)
Summer only

HENRY VIII NIGHT

This is really a "borderline" kind of theatre — those who attend this medieval banquet are actually participating in what gradually becomes a rollicking spree, where people don't remain strangers very long.

On Henry VIII nights, The Buttery Theatre Restaurant is transformed into the great dining hall at Henry's court, where you are transported back to the year 1530 A.D., when the most popular form of entertainment was The Banquet. The entire spectacle is controlled by the Court Steward, who welcomes the King, tastes his food, announces the program, and assures us that the "wretched prisoners in the dungeon get the leftovers."

Then, with great fanfare you will partake of wines, ale and mead; The First Remove includes broth with vegetables; The Second Remove, chicken filled with pâté, roast young pig and salad; The Third Remove, trifle with sherry, syllabub; The Fourth Remove brings us to Cheshire, Wiltshire and Somerset cheeses, apples and hearthcakes. In true Henry period fashion, the only table implements used are knives, wooden spoons, wooden dishes — and your fingers.

During the course of this toothsome repast you will be entertained by musicians, jugglers and court jesters.

For information and reservations, call The Buttery. $35 per couple — $17.50 single.

The Buttery, 19 Queen Street (468-2564)
October to May, Thursday through Saturday; June to September, alternate nights with the upstairs cabaret.

Shaw-related productions are presented at the Court House Theatre

UPSTAIRS AT THE BUTTERY

If you're looking for cabaret entertainment on a summer's evening, visit the Buttery, where you can enjoy a review comparable to Toronto's Theatre in the Dell. Popular stage personalities such as Tom Kneebone, Sandra O'Neill and Dinah Christie. star in shows written and produced especially for The Buttery.

Shows are held in the upstairs Banquet Room at a cost of $5 per person, and reservations are necessary.

19 Queen Street (468-2564)
June to September, Tuesday through Saturday, 9 p.m., Friday and Saturday, also at 11:30 p.m.

THE CANADIAN MIME THEATRE

Mime Theatre, once considered a fading European tradition, is thriving at Niagara-on-the-Lake, thanks to Brian Doherty and Adrian Pecknold, founders of The Canadian Mime Theatre.

Trained in mime in Paris, Pecknold conceived the idea of this theatre in 1969 while appearing at the Stratford Festival. Together with Doherty and Harro Maskow, a renowned mimist, he organized 100 performances during the first summer in an old fire hall.

Later, they moved to an old cinema, converted by Peter John Stokes, and renamed the Royal George. The theatre now boasts a Georgian facade of white and gold, a free-standing spiral staircase in the lobby, and the traditional black and white decor of pantomime.

Maskow's company has toured every province of Canada, and visited cities in the United States, Europe and Bulgaria. They have also given a series of outdoor concerts with the Canadian Brass throughout the Niagara Peninsula, and have performed for five seasons in Toronto.

In 1972, the Canadian Mime School was established at the theatre — the first of its kind in Canada. Currently under the direction of Wayne Pritchett, it attracts students from all over the continent for a six-month intensive course in mime technique. This includes acrobatics, juggling, the study of mask, improvisation, and the mastery of the unicycle (no easy feat!). The classes are small, and the ages vary, but students generally have university or drama school background. Once a week youth classes for 9 to 17 year olds are held as well. The study of mime is not only useful for the stage, but has also been excellent training for folk singers and language teachers.

Ticket prices: Adults, $5 evenings, $2.50 matinees; students and senior citizens, $3 evenings; children to age 14, $1.75 matinees. Saturday evenings, all seats are $5.

The Royal George, 83 Queen Street (468-3942)
May 28 to September 4
Matinees: Wednesday, Saturday and Sunday, 2 p.m.
Evenings: Tuesday to Saturday, 9 p.m.

Mime Theatre at the recently restored Royal George Theatre

8. Enjoying Niagara outdoors

Being outdoors is one of the best things about visiting Niagara-on-the-Lake. You can stroll through one of the area's many attractive parks, attend an art show or outdoor concert, enjoy the Peach Festival, have a workout on the golf links, or take your youngsters to a pet show, sailing or picnicking. Learn more about these on the following pages.

NIAGARA-ON-THE-LAKE PUBLIC PARKS

Some days are perfect for simply taking off to the nearest park and relaxing in nature. Here are some parks you might like to visit in the area.

Simcoe Park

Bordering the town's main streets, Simcoe Park is complete with playground equipment, wading pool, picnic tables, drinking fountain, and even a band on Sunday afternoons.
Picton and King Streets

Queen's Royal Park

On the site of the once proud Queen's Royal Hotel, this park overlooks the lake and includes beaches and picnic tables.
Front and King Streets

Memorial Park

Memorial was established in 1949 by the Royal Canadian Legion. It contains a playground, two tennis courts, a baseball diamond and swimming pool.
King Street

Ryerson Park

This lakeshore park is being eroded by water. There is a small beach, but little left of the park.
Niagara Boulevard

Newark Park

Open, rolling land, as yet undeveloped, it is open to the public and a nice place to picnic in warm weather.
Lakeshore Road

KERRY'S KITCHEN

Speaking of parks (and by inference, picnics), why not let Judy MacLachlan make you an unforgettable luncheon to take along? She's the imaginative owner of Kerry's Kitchen, and will help you plan a basket luncheon of cold pâté, chicken, freshly baked bread, cherry tomatoes, fruit and lemonade. Her choices for dinner include cold soup, chicken, cheddar cheese, marinated vegetables and cookies. Dinners cost $6.50; lunches, $3.50.

Three days' notice is required for

Simcoe Park

large preparations, and picnics for children's birthday parties can be arranged a day in advance.

Kerry's Kitchen also supplies snacks for bus tours leaving town after a theatre performance. Her rates vary with the size of the group.

(468-3443)
Open all year; available days, Monday through Saturday

THE NIAGARA GOLF COURSE

This picturesque, nine-hole course ranges along the shores of Lake Ontario and the Niagara River, with Fort Mississauga in its center.

Golfing is permitted from 7 a.m. until dark between April and October, and you can rent equipment for $5 weekdays, $6 weekends. If you wish to join, ask for the rate sheet at the course or write to the address below.

Plans are afoot to move the Golf Course in the 1980s to the Military Common near the Shaw Theatre, at which time the present site and Fort Mississauga will become public parkland.

143 Front Street (468-3424)

POOCH AND PET SHOW

This annual spring event is an extraordinary attraction originated by Gwen O'Loughlin, one of the town's animal lovers. Every year on the first Saturday in June, the local lovable creatures are brought together to be appreciated, and each entry justly receives a ribbon. Hamsters waive their usual preference for running their nocturnal wheels and perform by daylight. Tortoises, rabbits, snakes and snails are there in all their glory. They may not have a specific class, but they all have "class."

With dramatic flair, Gwen arranges a large performance ring decorated with fresh flowers and ten or more judges are in attendance as the fascinated audience chooses its favorite.

For more information, call 468-3188.
Simcoe Park
Picton and King Streets

THE OUTDOOR ART SHOW
on Queen Street

On the third Saturday and Sunday in June, the length of Queen Street becomes an art gallery. The show, produced by the Niagara-on-the-Lake Art Society, adds extra color to the area as local art is set up on easels or leaned against buildings or lamp posts, and artists patiently watch the strolling crowds hoping for a sale.

Over 100 entries of paintings, oils and watercolors, and photography vie for prizes awarded by two judges — one an artist, one a celebrity. Cash, award certificates or ribbons are given for first, second place and honorable mention. Artists' entrance fee is $5, browsing is free.

For information, write the Niagara-on-the-Lake Art Society, Box 764, Niagara-on-the-Lake.

NIAGARA PEACH FESTIVAL

In recent years, Niagara's large, ripening peach crop has warranted an August festival. (It's the fifth largest peach producing area in North America.) A Peach Queen is chosen, orchards are toured, pie-baking contests are held, and there is a special picnic in

Simcoe Park.

Although it's not yet as large as the Niagara Falls Grape Festival, the Peach Festival is quickly becoming a special event around mid-August. Admission is free.

THE VIRGIL STAMPEDE

Every Victoria Day weekend, the Virgil Stampede, with its color, excitement, and magnificent horse show, draws participants from the entire province. In country fair atmosphere, features include games of chance, fireworks, puppet shows, model flying, rides, candy floss and hot dogs; there are top-notch Western and English horsemanship displays and competitions as well as a bake sale and craft show. Admission is $1 for adults, children under 15, free.

At the Virgil Arena, 3½ miles from the Clocktower in Niagara.
(See map on page 115).

ESPECIALLY FOR SAILORS

Gillingham's Yacht Basin

Gillingham's Yacht Basin is a favorite gathering place in summer, with yachtsmen scurrying about in nautical gear and sails snapping in the wind.

Increasing numbers of visitors arrive in Niagara-on-the-Lake by yacht to pick up one of Kerry's picnics (See Kerry's Kitchens, page *86*) to serve on board, have a fine dinner at an inn, or enjoy an evening at the theatre before heading back to "sea." Berths, incidentally, should be reserved well in advance of arrival. Their business is primarily dockage, storage and repair — rentals are not available.

Niagara Dockside (468-3224)

Junior Sailing

Gillingham's offers a four-week course in basic sailing in July, and another in August, for ages 10 to 16. Cost of each series is $65.

Lessons take place on both Lake Ontario and the Niagara River. The club meets in an A-frame building across from the Anchorage behind Gillingham's Yacht Basin. Call 468-3224 for more information.

Seneca Cruises

Charter cruises may be arranged at Gillingham's. A two-masted schooner is available for cruises from 1½ to three hours, seven days a week in summer, by reservation. Choose between daytime or sunset sailing.
(468-7834)

R.C.Y.C. Regatta

The Royal Canadian Yacht Club in Toronto holds a popular regatta in Niagara-on-the-Lake each summer. Dates vary, so call 468-3224 for more specific information.

The Stores

The old and new truly meet here. This nautical centre is a remnant of days of hardier travel, located in the old Niagara Street Railway Co. powerhouse.

But it still carries everything the modern yachtsman needs, from spars and rigging, foul weather gear, and boat shoes to gift and luxury items.

48 John Street, in the rear, across from the Pillar and Post (468-2101)
Monday to Saturday, 9 a.m. to 6 p.m.

The Yacht Basin, a favorite summer gathering place

9. Inns and restaurants

Niagara-on-the-Lake is one of those special places blessed with a number of excellent places to eat and charming places to stay, often right under one roof. Here are our choices, and also some restaurants to look for, if you take the out-trips to Youngstown and Lewiston, N.Y., suggested in a later chapter:

THE PILLAR AND POST

Originally a cannery, The Pillar and Post is now the largest inn in town, with a high-ceilinged dining room, craft shop, a working forge, a small workshop theatre, a hand-weaving studio, a pub and the Fireplace Lounge, a popular meeting place with lively music in a welcoming atmosphere of copper color and old brick.

The dining room menu features duck à l'orange, fresh salmon and rack of lamb as specialties, while The Pillar Pub downstairs features prime ribs of beef. Dinners run from $7 to $12 and Sunday brunch is $5.

Recently, the inn has been expanded to include 60 air-conditioned rooms, a sauna, whirlpool bath, fitness club, conference and exhibit areas for conventions. Each room is decorated in Early Canadian style with furniture made at the inn. All suites and some rooms contain fireplaces.

In winter, The Pillar and Post is a favorite refuge for bridge buffs and others on retreat from city life, offering excellent food, entertainment, a health club, or the privacy to simply curl up with a good book.

Bicycles are available for rent at $2.50 per half day and $5 a full day.

Room rates: $33 — single
41 — double
45 — double with fireplace

48 John Street (468-2123) from Toronto (361-1931)
MC, Chx, AmEx, DC

THE PRINCE OF WALES HOTEL

Originally built in the late 1800s to accommodate stagecoach and steamship passengers, Long's Hotel was renamed The Prince of Wales in 1901 to honor Edward VII's visit to Canada. With the new addition made in 1975, there are now 40 rooms.

The dining room is quietly elegant with bottle-green walls and fresh flowers on white tablecloths. A greenhouse dining area overlooks Simcoe Park. A fireplace gives the lounge-bar a comfortable, softly lit appeal. Dining facilities for up to 140 persons are provided in banquet rooms.

Luncheons range from omelettes or

By the dining room hearth at the Pillar and Post

RESTAURANTS

1. Oban Inn
2. Gate House
3. Le Doux Little Angel
4. Angel Inn
5. Pillar and Post
6. The Buttery
7. Brassbounds Cafe
8. Prince of Wales
9. The Parkview
10. Crepe Susy's
11. The Bean Pot

quiche at $3.75 to trout and steak at $4.95. Dinner entries range from veal or breast of chicken in wine for $6.25 to the deluxe scampi la croix for $11.50.

Room rates: $33 — single (summer)
27 — single (winter)
37 — double (summer)
32 — double (winter)
35 and $50 daily —
banquet rooms

6 Picton Street (468-3246)
MC, Chx, AmEx

THE OBAN INN

The Oban Inn and restaurant occupies a large colonial house touched with the elegance of Victorian England. Built in 1824, it was once a private home belonging to a Scottish captain named Malloy, whose ghost is said to still linger here.

Edna Burroughs, the present owner, offers fresh flowers daily in the five attractive dining rooms, which can accommodate as many as 400 people at three sittings. A cheery sunroom off the dining area offers a view of the lake, while the verandah overlooking the gardens is a favorite spot to enjoy lunch on a sunny day. In winter, the verandah is converted to a glassed-in garden.

A luncheon buffet table in the Lamp Room features steak-and-kidney pie, devilled eggs, and salad. A complete dinner is available for $7.50; steak, sole, or lobster à la carte are offered from $8.50. Dessert specialties include Meringue chantilly, strawberry mousse, and pie à la mode.

Prince of Wales Hotel

The Oban Inn

In the evening, there is music around the piano, and newcomers are welcomed by Edna's son, Gary, who now manages the Inn.

While you're in the piano bar, look for the gallery of signed photographs of Shaw Festival Theatre stars, who often frequent the Oban for after-theatre parties. It's a good idea to reserve a room in advance, if you plan to stay — there are 20 rooms of varying degrees of luxury.

Room rates: $20 — single
　　　　　25 — twin
　　　　　30 — front room
　　　　　　　 overlooking lake
　　　　　35 — apartment

160 Front Street (468-7811)
MC, Chx, AmEx, DC

OBAN HOUSE

Oban House is a large renovated house adjoining the spacious inn to accommodate up to 20 conferees at meetings and seminars. The rooms, freshly decorated with chintz, feature private baths, private bars and dining rooms; and a knotty pine board room is available for meetings. Summer evenings will find visitors on the screened porch overlooking the lake. Reservations for Oban House can be made at the Oban Inn.

Room rate: $30

160 Front Street (468-7811)
MC, Chx, AmEx

THE ANGEL INN

The simple exterior of The Angel Inn disguises a cozy, nostalgic atmosphere within. Built in 1779, it was host to General Brock and his men, and Governor Simcoe. After the town was razed 34 years later, it rose once again to become an inn. Ten rooms accommodate guests, with one unique room boasting a "fertility bed." Decor is authentically Early Canadian with low, rough-hewn beams and shuttered windows, four-poster beds, beautifully preserved quilts, and antique tapestries.

On your arrival, you'll be welcomed by T.J. LeDoux, the friendly proprietor. A glowing fire awaits in winter, and an antique piano provides old-time music on weekends. You'll also enjoy T.J.'s display of old war relics, teapots, clocks and uniforms in glass cases in the dining room.

The menu offers a wide variety at lunch and dinner, as well as after the theatre — from a vegetarian plate for $4.95 to queen crab for $9.75, or the chateaubriand bouquetière for two, a house specialty.

Room rate: $22 — single
          25 — double
224 Regent Street (468-3411)
MC, Chx, AmEx, DC

THE ANCHORAGE

The outdoor patio lounge at The Anchorage is a popular spot to watch sailboats preparing to enter or leave the harbor on a summer evening. Many yachtsmen also seek refuge here on stormy nights when they prefer not to sleep aboard. The motel offers accommodation with air-conditioning, color TV, and entertainment.

Sandwiches and snacks are served in the nautically decorated lounge during the afternoon hour when hotel dining rooms are often closed.

Winter rates: $17 double
Summer rates: $23 double
186 Ricardo Street (468-2141)

THE BUTTERY THEATRE RESTAURANT

The Buttery is a restaurant, cabaret theatre, and home of Henry VIII Night (see Theatres — Great and Small) — all products of owners Margaret and Fritz Niemann's creative imaginations.

The Buttery's outdoor terrace overlooks the street, and is a favorite people-watching site. Here you can linger over tea or a cool drink in warm weather, while inside, a more intimate atmosphere is encouraged with dinner served by candlelight. The menu includes such specialties as pheasant imperial and la terrine de Strassbourg, a truffled goose liver and one of Joan of Arc's favorites. Afternoon tea of scones, cakes, sandwiches and homemade strawberry jam is hefty and delicious, a real treat for only $2.75.

Gourmets will appreciate a special service offering French cuisine especially prepared — all that's required is two days' notice. You can enjoy, either at home or in The Buttery, such delights as rack of lamb for $10, roast sirloin with truffles for $10.50 or poached lobster for $14.

Reservations are requested for dinner, Henry VIII Night and the theatre.

19 Queen Street (468-2564)
Daily noon to 5 p.m., 9 p.m. to midnight
MC, Chx, DC

THE BEAN POT

Moffat Mews, a new shopping area, offers two new restaurants with unique menus, The Bean Pot and Crêpe Susy's.

The Bean Pot, on the lower level, features large black kettles of steaming pea or beef and barley soups for $1.69. Main courses include pioneer stew for $2.49, steak sandwich for $1.49, or baked beans with smoked sausage for $1.89. For dessert, there's cinnamon baked apple for only 69¢.

60 Picton Street (468-2983)
May 1 to September 30, daily 9 a.m. to midnight
October 1 to April 30, daily except Wednesdays, 11 a.m. to 7 p.m.

CRÊPE SUSY'S

Crêpe Susy's on the upper level is brighter, with a more delicate atmosphere. Settle into one of the white wrought-iron chairs and order salad; a seafood crêpe for $3.95; chicken à la king for $3.50; or one of several dessert crêpes for $1.50.

May 1 to September 30, daily 9 a.m. to midnight
October 1 to April 30, daily except Mondays, noon to 8 p.m.

BRASSBOUND'S CAFE

"Country fresh and crispy clean" is owner Margaret Niemann's description of her new café. Designed to attract the after-theatre crowd, it features hamburgers, sandwiches and snacking foods until the wee hours.

13 Queen Street (468-3053)
Tuesday to Thursday, 11 a.m. to 9 p.m.; Friday and Saturday, 11 a.m. to 3 a.m. Sunday 11 a.m. to 3 p.m.

PARKVIEW RESTAURANT

If you're travelling with children or looking for a quick, informal meal, stop in at the Parkview. Despite its humble exterior, the food is good and the nautical decor neat as a pin. Sandwiches and hamburgers start at $1.50, and fish and chips is a favorite at $3.50. There's also a take-out counter.

16 Picton Street (468-9928)
May to October, daily except Mondays, 7 a.m. to 8 p.m.
November to April, daily except Mondays, 7 a.m. to 5 p.m.

LEDOUX' LITTLE ANGEL

T.J. LeDoux of The Angel Inn also owns this creatively decorated restaurant, with an 1800s printing press in the corner, sewing machines converted to tables, and a fireplace in the bar. A new dinner menu is in preparation. Luncheon offerings include beef on a bun for $1.50, steak sandwich for $2.25 and chicken or shrimp and chips for $2.50.

58 Queen Street (468-7370)
Daily 11:30 a.m. to 2:30 p.m., 3:30 p.m. to 8 p.m.
Chx, MC, AmEx

IN YOUNGSTOWN

THE OLD FORT INN

Just south of Fort Niagara, this recently remodelled restaurant features steaks, prime rib, homemade soups, and fresh baked bread. There's a steak sandwich special for $5.25. A lunch-time fashion show is held every Wednesday from noon to 2 p.m. Fridays and Saturdays offer entertainment between 9:30 p.m. and 1:30 a.m.

110 Main Street (716-745-7456)
Monday to Friday, 11:30 a.m. to 3 p.m., 5 p.m. to 10 p.m.; Saturday, 11:30 a.m. to 3 p.m., 4 p.m. to 11 p.m.; Sundays, summers only, 11:30 a.m. to 3 p.m., 5 p.m. to 10 p.m.
All credit cards

IN LEWISTON

CLARKSON HOUSE

A well-known restaurant whose renowned steak and lobster draws clientele all the way from Toronto, Clarkson House's open grill offers steaks ranging from $7.40 to $8.75; a twin feast of lobster is $17, and you can finish off with cherries jubilee, or baked Alaska, both under $2. Reservations are advised.

810 Center Street (716-754-4544)
Daily except Mondays, 5 p.m. to 1 a.m.
No credit cards

DONNA FELICIA'S

A haven for Italian food lovers, Donna Felicia's is divided into cozy rooms and combines an intimate atmosphere with such tempting entrées as spaghetti, lasagne, manicotti, fettuccine, and seafood. For $8.25 to $10 you can order a steak dinner or go all the way with lobster tails for $11.50.

490 Center Street (716-754-7901)
Bankamericard, AmEx, MC

MOORADIAN'S COAT OF ARMS

Across the road from Donna Felicia's, this Armenian restaurant features some unique dishes for the area. A favorite for lunch is the blue-cheeseburger at $1.50, and each table is adorned with a barrel of dill pickles. For a fixed price of $7.95, you can feast on stuffed grape leaves with rice, shish-kebab, salad, Armenian bread, bourma (thin layers of dough with crushed nuts and syrup) and Armenian coffee.

425 Center Street (716-754-8674)
Daily, 11 a.m. to 1 a.m.
No credit cards

RIVERSIDE INN

This restaurant has both an upstairs room, decorated like a captain's cabin in wood trim with leather chairs, and a downstairs room with a Mississippi ferryboat atmosphere, and menus on paddles. Dinners range from top sirloin for $6.25 to lobster tails for $12.50. Try their cheesecake specialty at 95¢.

115 South Water Street (716-754-8206)
Lounge — Monday to Saturday, 4 p.m. to midnight; Sundays 1 p.m. to midnight
Restaurant — Monday to Thursday, 5:30 p.m. to 10 p.m.; Friday and Saturday to midnight; Sunday, 1 p.m. to 10 p.m.
All major credit cards

10. Out-tripping

NIAGARA RIVER PARKWAY TO NIAGARA FALLS

A drive along the Niagara River Parkway offers a scenic natural shoreline with trees, gardens, and picnic areas along the way. Historic sites are well marked by the Niagara Parks Commission.

This drive to Niagara Falls via the Parkway focuses on the best things to see and tries to help you skirt the gaudy tourist areas.

Begin at Queens Parade Road (beside the Shaw Festival Theatre). Just before setting off, you might like to stop at the end of Queen's Parade at the Kurtz Fruit Stand to pick up some fruit and vegetables to nibble on along the way. Then, follow the road along the Parkway, where you will pass McFarland House and Field House (see Museums). Inniskillin Wines is next, the smallest winery in Canada, but already possessing a reputation for high quality wines. There are no formal tours, but you can see the fruitlands at closer range if you stop at their winery shop. (262-4375) A mile or so farther, the Wayside Chapel appears to the right. Built in 1966 by volunteers from the Christian Reformed Church, it holds only six people at a time and is open daily from 6 a.m. to 10 p.m. all year. A taped devotional message and organ music

are offered inside, as well as a Bible for use there. Thousands of visitors sign the guest book every year, and it's a favorite site for wedding pictures.

A short distance ahead the road curves around the village of Queenston and up the sharp incline of Queenston Heights, site of General Brock's famous battle. At the top of the hill is Queenston Heights Park, where you can visit the huge monument to Brock, stop in at the Queenston Heights Restaurant, or take in one of the free Sunday afternoon concerts at the new Bandshell. They can be heard at 2:30 p.m. from the end of June to the end of August. Or you might enjoy a game of tennis on the public courts. Cost is $2 an hour, and reservations are needed in summer. Call 262-5109.

From the entrance to the park you can see the gates of the Queenston-Lewiston Bridge. Opened in November 1962, it links Canada's Queen Elizabeth Way with the New York Thruway.

Around the bend in the road is the well known floral clock, a combined effort of Ontario Hydro and the Niagara Parks Commission. The floral face, which can be filled with as many as 24,000 plants, is constantly in

Spanish Aero Car

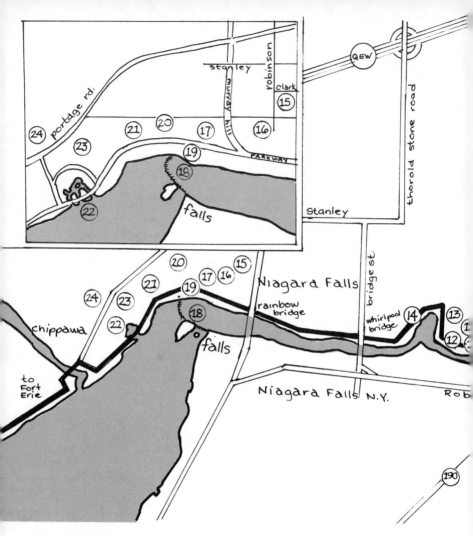

OUT-TRIPPING — NIAGARA PARKWAY

1	McFarland House	7	Queenston Heights Bandshell
2	Field House	8	Queenston-Lewiston Bridge
3	Inniskillin Wines	9	Floral Clock
4	Wayside Chapel	10	Sir Adam Beck Hydro Plant
5	Queenston Heights Restaurant	11	School of Horticulture
6	Brock's Monument	12	Niagara Glen Restaurant

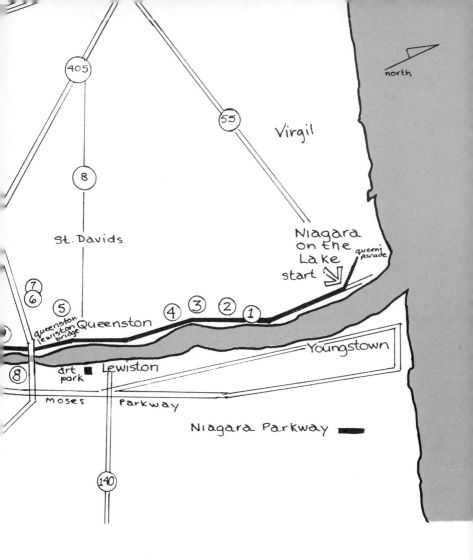

McFarland House

colorful bloom during the growing season.

Beyond the clock loom the towers and powerhouse of the Sir Adam Beck Generating Station, one of the major hydro producers for Ontario and parts of New York state. Directly across the gorge is a good view of its American counterpart, the Robert Moses Generating Station.

A short way up the road, watch for the Niagara School of Horticulture, a low, modern building with experimental gardens. Established in 1936 by the Parks Commission, it is the only school of its kind in North America, its graduates becoming teachers, researchers, or park executives. The school also cultivates land to supply superior nursery stock to the park system, a high priority throughout the 35-mile parkland.

At this point on the river bank, the Niagara Glen provides a pathway into the gorge down to the river's edge. This is a favorite area for hikers, botanists, geologists and river lovers, but caution is recommended, as the violent turbulence of the water below the Falls can be seen at close range (without railings) as well as layers of exposed, ancient rock. Rare plants continue to grow here, protected in the gorge from civilization.

After the strenuous climb back to the top, you might wish to stop at the Glen Restaurant for some refreshment.

Bordering the gardening school is the Whirlpool Golf Course, a public green open from April to November. Open seven days a week, the cost is $8 before 4 p.m., $6 after. Rentals are available. There is a clubhouse with a

A spectacular boat ride

small restaurant overlooking the course.

Another bend in the road leads to the Spanish Aero Car over the Whirlpool Rapids. The longest suspended railway in the world, it offers an awesome ride over a churning whirlpool in the lower part of the river. Its 1800-foot cables and open car were built by a Spanish company in 1916, and are now operated by the Parks Commission. Carrying 40 passengers at a time, it operates at a height of 250 feet above the water. The whirlpool is caused by a drop in the river bed of 60 feet in less than half a mile. At this point, the channel between the cliffs is 300 feet. The car is in operation from May to October. Rates for adults are $1.60, teens $1, and children 75¢.

Now, you are entering Niagara Falls, and the Parkway will curve along the embankment and its stone wall to Queen Victoria Park and the brink of Horseshoe Falls. Watch for signs for the Maid of the Mist ride and the Scenic Tunnels under the Falls. The Maid of the Mist is a ferry carrying passengers to the very base of the cataract. Passengers wear hooded raincoats on this half-hour tour. From mid-May to mid-October, the boat leaves every 15 minutes daily. Adult rates are $3, children 75¢, under 6 years, free.

The Tunnels are entered by elevators carrying viewers 125 feet down through solid rock to the three open portals with a view of the pounding waters from beneath. Raincoats and hoods are provided for this year-round attraction as well. Rates are: adults, $2.10, children 75¢, under 7 years, 25¢, senior citizens groups, $1.25 per person.

Looming over Queen Victoria Park are two towers: the Skylon with its outside elevator, which can be directly reached by a road, and the Panasonic Tower, with access by elevated railway. If you're wondering which Tower to visit, here's a run-down on what each has to offer:

The Panasonic has a dolphin and sea lion show, Burning Springs Wax Museum, a dining room at the top, and a summer "waltzing waters" show. Tower admission is $2 for adults, $1.25 for students and senior citizens, and 75¢ for children. It's open from 9 a.m. to 9 p.m.

The newer, more dramatic Skylon offers boutiques on two floors, entertainment, a revolving dining room, and the largest indoor ferris wheel in the world. Tower admission is $2.75 for adults, $1.25 for students and senior citizens, and $1 for children.

The Parks Commission Greenhouse offers a free spectacular exhibition in all seasons, and is open seven days a week from 9:30 a.m. to 4:30 p.m. Oakes Garden and amphitheatre nearby is an example of how the Greenhouse plants are placed in formal settings. Admission is also free.

Dufferin Islands would be a nature lover's delight in any setting, but here in the midst of this commercial tourist area, its serenity is a miracle. The Parks Commission has enhanced this small area near the rapids with nature trails and tumbling streams. It is open free to the public from May to

Paddle boats at Dufferin Islands

108

October, where children can use the wading pool and paddleboats ($1.50) or follow wooden footpaths over streams.

Oak Hall — on Portage Road high on a hill overlooking Queen Victoria Park — was once the dream home of Sir Harry Oakes, an American who made his fortune in gold in Ontario. It now belongs to the Parks Commission and is open to the public in summer and used for art shows. The lawns have been converted to a Par 3 golf course, open April to November, with rentals available. Fees are: 18 holes, $2.75; 9 holes, $2.25; children $2. It can be reached from the Park through Dufferin Islands.

Across the road from Oak Hall is Marineland and Game Farm. A full day's entertainment for children and adults, it offers 75 acres full of marine life and wild animals, including whales, porpoises, seals and farm animals, deer, buffalo, llamas, lynx and lions, to name a few. It's open all year.

As a final stop on your drive, look for the Old Stone Inn on Robinson Street near the Skylon. This inn and restaurant was once a tombstone factory, but the old stones now house a quaint beamed bar and dining room, with huge fireplaces and a congenial atmosphere. You'll enjoy dining and relaxing here before returning to the serenity of Niagara-on-the-Lake. A new three-storey section contains 115 rooms with bath, sliding glass doors, some with fireplaces. The front treed courtyard at the entrance leads to a glass-enclosed lobby, through which can be seen another landscaped courtyard with a swimming pool at the rear. Here a licenced patio lounge offers cool drinks, refreshment and summer luncheons. The glass lobby also leads to the rustic dining room where old stone, a huge fireplace, heavy beamed ceiling with massive chandeliers, a wall of books, and even a minstrel gallery invite you to enjoy fine fare in dramatic style. An added attraction at dinner is the sumptuous salad bar.

On the lower level, a soft brown bar, again with huge fireplace, old stone and weathered wood, welcomes you for drinks and light lunches. Telephone the Inn at 357-1234; Restaurant, 357-1166.

YOUNGSTOWN AND LEWISTON, N.Y.

Youngstown By Boat

On the opposite bank of the Niagara River lies Youngstown, New York, Niagara-on-the-Lake's American counterpart, with its own unique attractions.

Youngstown shares the same colonial atmosphere as Niagara-on-the-Lake, with its great shuttered houses and ominous fort from yesterday coexisting with today's peaceful community. But the town's personality is noticeably different, flavored by American colonial taste rather than Niagara's British influence. Even the interpretation of history is different on this side of the river. For years there has been a continuing debate surrounding the background and events of the War of 1812, with school texts

Horseshoe Falls at Niagara

Fort Niagara, Niagara-on-the-Lake

and historical plaques on both sides in occasional disagreement.

Probably the easiest way to get to Youngstown — and the most fun — is to take the passenger ferry across from Niagara. The open launch, large enough to carry a dozen people, runs approximately every half hour between May and September in the afternoon and by request at other times.

You must push the button on a post at the dock near the Canada Customs office to activate a light signal, alerting the operator that a customer is waiting. After a five-minute crossing past anchored yachts and within view of two imposing forts, the ferry deposits its passengers on the Youngstown dock, beside the Yacht Club. Immigration officers wait in a small office nearby, but they are congenial and relaxed, in keeping with the casual nature of this unique international border.

A short steep climb up either a wooden stairway or a winding paved road brings you to Main Street, Youngstown. You won't need a car as

the town is easy to explore on foot.

Comerford's Riverview Inn on Main Street offers refreshment with a drink at its rustic bar, or an inexpensive seafood meal in the dining room overlooking the yacht basin below, where you can view the yachts bobbing against the sunset.

A quarter of a mile north of the Riverview is Fort Niagara. Built by Louis XV's engineer in 1726, when French colonies in the New World were expanding, the stone fort was designed to resemble a French manor house, its height and location providing an excellent view of the lake and river basin. Local Indians were told during its construction that it was to be a trading post. But its thick stone walls, inside well and six-pounder battery soon made it obvious that it was a solid fortress.

Brigadier-General John Prideaux, a British army officer with a French name, captured the fort from the French during the war between England and France in 1759. Prideaux was killed in battle and Sir William Johnson, British Superintendent of

Indian Affairs became Commandant of the fort until his death in 1774. Because Johnson was well loved by the local Iroquois they remained loyal to the British cause after his death. The names of Johnson and Prideaux are visible on street signs in Niagara-on-the-Lake, and many French names can be found on both sides of the border. The town of Lewiston, for instance, was named for King Louis XIV of France.

When the American Revolution began, Fort Niagara became the scene of further warfare. From here, Butler's Rangers made their forays into enemy areas and Loyalist refugees fleeing the colonies streamed into its protective walls.

The Americans received the fort from the British by treaty after the Revolution in 1796, and used it as a base to attack Fort George in the War of 1812.

Taken back by the British the following year, it was returned to American hands and remained so ever since.

One of the special sights here is the "Castle" or barracks designed like a stone manor house. This has been refurnished in Louis XV style. The Castle's well has only recently been uncovered and rumor has it that it's haunted.

You can also examine the hot shot battery with its furnace for heating cannon balls, as well as old stone buildings whose masonry is the oldest in northern United States.

Fort Niagara is open daily from 9 a.m. to 4:30 p.m. in winter, and from 9 a.m. to dusk in summer. Admission is $1 for adults; children under 12 are free. Phone 716-745-7611 for more information.

A second way to reach Youngstown is by car, taking the Queenston-Lewiston bridge on the Niagara Parkway through the town of Lewiston, New York.

This picturesque American town shares with Niagara-on-the-Lake the privilege of housing a new and beautiful theatre. Artpark, although modern in design, is very different in style from the Shaw Theatre. Built on a spectacular hillside at the end of

Portage Road, its great covered amphitheatre is open from mid-June to mid-September. Programs include the symphony, ballet, folk and modern dance, rock bands and "pop" concerts, with featured performers such as Van Cliburn, the Joffrey Ballet and Metropolitan Opera stars.

Some picnic lovers spread tablecloths complete with wine bottle, long-stemmed glasses and cheese. On a warm evening you can sit on the grass above the stage for a nominal $3. Inside seats are $4. The ticket office in season can be reached at 716-754-4375. Off-season, you can call the Executive Director in Youngstown at 754-3377.

Lewiston's Center Street has a number of excellent restaurants and boutiques. You can read more about restaurants under Inns and Restaurants, but as we pass them, they include the Clarkson House, Donna Felicia's, Mooradian's Coat of Arms, and the Riverside Inn.

Before or after dining, why not browse in some of the interesting shops on Center Street: there's the Lewiston Country Store for early American reproductions; Sister and Brother for children's togs; Quote and Quill for stationery and cards; and the Wood Loft in the old opera house for crafts, antiques, toys, and wooden bowls. Tiffany House, a specialty shop located in a large old home, displays gifts, lamps, and bathroom accessories. It's open Monday through Friday from 9 a.m. to 5 p.m. and Saturdays until 6.

At the old Lewiston library on Center Street, Temperance and Tea offers lunch, snacks and tea in quaint surroundings.

Hansen's Fish Market open year round at the foot of Portage, off Center, sells a variety of seafood and offers fish and chips to eat in or take out for the traveller in a hurry.

If you drive along the river road from Lewiston back to Youngstown you can observe the old homes above the embankment — many are restored with real flair. Then, backtrack along the river to return to Lewiston and the Lewiston-Queenston Bridge.

QUEENSTON, ST. DAVIDS, AND VIRGIL

Bordering Niagara-on-the-Lake to the south are three small villages which have played a prominent role in the early history of Upper Canada. Once bustling commercial centres, these quiet farm communities are found today in the heart of Ontario's fruitland. All three once showed promise of a burgeoning future: Queenston as an international port and postal depot, St. Davids and Virgil as milling and distribution centres. The quirks of history brought about their sudden eclipse.

We'll begin with some background on Queenston before you set out exploring.

* * * * *

The early pioneers arriving from Fort Niagara during the American Revolution, and later by ship from Toronto and Kingston, chose to settle here because of its proximity to the Niagara River and the natural flats or

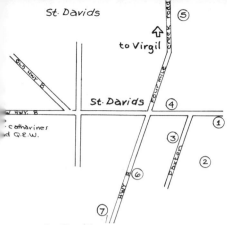

St. Davids

1. United Church
2. Golf Course
3. Locust Hall
4. Presbyterian Church
5. Cannery
6. Reflections of Tyme
7. Indian Burial Ground

Queenston

1. Willowbank
2. Brock Memorial Church
3. Something Different
4. Public Library
5. Laura Secord House
6. South Landing Crafts
7. William Lyon MacKenzie House

"landing" for boats on its shore. Known originally as "The Landing" or "West Landing", the settlement became, within a year or two, the focus of navigation on the Niagara River. Supplies and goods were portaged from this point overland to Lake Erie.

Governor Simcoe chose this site in 1792 to build several barracks for his Queen's Rangers. He renamed the village, Queen's Town, probably in honor of the military corps, but this was soon shortened to Queenston. The Governor also established a ferry service to Fort Niagara and set a tariff of tolls for both military personnel and residents. In 1802 a postal distribution office was created to handle mail travelling to the interior. It was the first such office in Upper Canada.

Robert Hamilton, one of the first settlers here, became a prosperous merchant in the small community and a leader in the town as it grew. In 1789 Hamilton was awarded the "portage rights" at the landing whereupon he established port facilities and dock warehousing to accommodate the growing international trade with the United States and Lower Canada. Soon the port was a hub of activity with overland trails radiating from it to Lake Erie and other settlements along the river. By the early 1800s as many as four vessels a day of 60-100 tons, and 60 wagons, were loading and unloading grain, livestock, lumber and military equipment.

The portage road from Queenston to Chippawa, muddy and rutted in summer, icy and snow-covered in winter, carried travellers and trade around the Falls. Goods were hauled

Hon. Robert Hamilton, founder of Queenston

over the Niagara escarpment by horse and wagon, and even sailing vessels as large as 10 tons were "portaged" from one lake to another via runners and oxen, to the delight of spectators who gathered from far and wide to watch.

In the midst of all this success, Robert Hamilton was able to acquire large tracts of land in the peninsula; his sons prospered as well in the shipbuilding industry. The cities of Hamilton and St. Catharines were named, after Robert's death for his family and his wife, Catharine.

The War of 1812 brought activity of another sort to Queenston. War supplies arrived at its wharves and troops billeted in its military camps. Eventually one of the major battles of the conflict took place on the heights beside the town. General Isaac Brock was killed here when he charged the heights to dislodge American soldiers from the summit. The enemy was defeated later in the day by Brock's successor, Major-General Roger Sheaffe with the aid of friendly Indians, and forced to surrender.

It was at this time, in late June of 1813, that Laura Second took her famous walk from Queenston to DeCew Falls. It came about when she overheard enemy soldiers billeted in her home, discussing a forthcoming attack. Setting out on foot to warn the Loyalist troops twenty miles away, she completed the difficult journey, and relayed her warning. Partly as a result of her effort, the battle at DeCew Falls or Beaverdams was won by the British.

By 1814, Queenston suffered as much at the hands of the withdrawing enemy forces as did Newark, with many buildings being burned to the ground. However, the town managed to recover quickly. By the 1820s there were 100 homes for 400-500 inhabitants, and 11 taverns within the village. In ten years time, steamers were routinely entering the port at Queenston and the horse-drawn railway between Queenston and Chippawa was in operation in 1839.

The Hamilton sons went into business building and owning steamboats and sent a steamer to Kingston and Montreal to bring mail to Queenston. Alexander Hamilton, as Postmaster and Sheriff of the town, regularly received three wagon loads of mail from the mailpacket steamer which were sorted and then distributed by stage coach.

Within a few years the town was eclipsed by the Welland Canal. The long portage route around the Falls needed an easier solution and the canal from Lake Ontario to Lake Erie was it. By the end of the 1830s, port facilities had become obsolete and population subsequently decreased.

In 1850, a suspension bridge from Queenston to Lewiston was erected. But neither bridge nor railway was able to save the commercial life of Queenston.

The steamer from Toronto maintained its run for many years but was used primarily for tourists and picnicers. Eventually in the latter half of the century, hotels and industries closed their doors for lack of business. Queenston became a quiet residential area, a centre for neighboring farmers, a sleepy village with one of the most dramatic landscapes in the world. It remains so today.

Because of the tragedy of the War of 1812, few historic buildings remain in the village. Robert Hamilton's impressive stone mansion on the embankment above the landing escaped the war but was ironically destroyed by fire shortly after.

Laura Secord's house still stands at Queenston and Partition Streets. It was damaged during the War of 1812 but rebuilt and later still, greatly altered. In 1969, the small Georgian frame building was purchased by Laura Secord Shops. Peter Stokes, restoration architect, returned it to its original condition and painted it yellow. The neat rectangular home, now authentically furnished, is a centre hall design with simple square windows on either side of the door. It is open in summer from May to October, Monday to Friday, 10 a.m. to 6 p.m., Saturday and Sunday, 10 a.m. to 7 p.m., and the Homestead Shop offers a selection of delicacies, ice creams and handcraft gift items. Admission is 25¢.

Brock Memorial Church, also known as St. Saviour's, is one of Queenston's monuments to the famous General, the town's "saviour." The compact, steep-roofed church, constructed in 1879, faces the river at Front Street, its six-sided steeple housing one of the oldest church bells in Ontario. It is constructed of grey Queenston limestone, brought in wagons from the quarry above.

There are several unique features about this church. First, it was dedicated to a layman by the founding parishioners, an unusual practice. The stained glass windows bear military symbols rather than religious

The Cayuga arrives. From an old postcard

ones and one window is dedicated to the York Volunteers who fought so bravely at Queenston Heights. Brock's coat of arms is also represented here in another of the windows.

The building itself is a copy of a Christopher Wren design. Wren, an English architect, lived from 1632-1723 and designed 52 churches in London noted for their elegance, clarity and fine spires, features which are also present in this graceful structure. The church is open to the public only at Sunday service.

"Willowbank", the mansion on the hill overlooking the village at Dee Road, was built in 1833-1834 by Alexander Hamilton, one of Robert's sons. An elegant example of Classic Revival style, the grey stone house

commands a magnificent view of village and river below. Each of its soaring white Ionic pillars is one solid piece of timber, cut from a neighboring farm, with hand-carved capitals and lifted into upright position by pulleys. Today the house is used as a convent by the Sisters of Charity and is not open to the public.

At the foot of the Heights, William Lyon MacKenzie lived in his grey stone Georgian house in the early 1820s. After partial destruction, the original stone was used to rebuild this 2-storey house, with a centre-hall plan, balanced and symmetrical. The rest was brought from Queenston Quarries. William Lyon MacKenzie King, the grandson of the former journalist-rebel, officially opened the

MacKenzie House

restored building in 1938. MacKenzie house has now been leased out as a private home and at the present time is closed to the public.

The Queenston Baptist Church on Queenston Street was constructed by the congregation in 1842, a rectangular stone building with pointed Gothic windows. It was used as a church until World War I and then by the Queenston Women's Institute until 1953. While under their tenure, the simple spire was removed. A local physician purchased the building in 1969 and gave it to the village as a Library and Community Centre.

A unique old structure stands at the corner of Front Street and Kent. Its frame exterior is weathered and unrestored but as one of Queenston's original inns, it dates back to 1850. Now, at the South Landing Crafts Centre, it's a weaver's delight; inside are looms and yarns for those interested in the art of hand weaving. Call 262-4216 if you'd like to visit.

Across from the Crafts Centre at the foot of Kent Street, a small park is being developed by the Niagara Parks Commission, to be ready in summer 1977. It will share a remarkable view of river gorge and the dramatic theatre, Artpark, on the opposite shore.

Another small shop on Queenston Street at Highlander is known as "Something Different." It features Canadian handcrafts by local women including crocheted afghans, pillows, knitted bedjackets and woollen caps,

View from Queenston Heights, 1920

unusual china and gifts. The shop is open six days a week from 9 a.m. to 5 p.m. (262-4927).

At Queenston Heights Park, on the escarpment overlooking the town, you'll see several markers commemorating the history of the famous battle. A walking tour map of the park, compiled by the Federal Government, is available inside the entrance way to Brock's monument, open daily in summer from May to Labor Day.

The park comprises 110 acres of land dominated by the towering second monument to General Brock. The first, erected in 1824 was destroyed by raiders in April, 1840. Rebuilt between 1853 - 1856, it stands 196 feet high. Beneath are buried Brock and MacDonnell, his aide-de-camp. From the top of the circular stairway in the monument you'll see a magnificent panorama of the Niagara River rushing to join Lake Ontario, with orchards and vineyards stretching for miles.

Other markers in or near the park are the stone cenotaph placed by H.R.H. Albert Edward, Prince of Wales, in September 1860, on the spot where Brock fell. There is also a cut stone memorial at the edge of the escarpment, erected by the Government of Canada in 1910 in honor of Laura Ingersoll Secord. An irregular piece of Queenston limestone, erected in 1932 by the Niagara Parks Commission, marks the site of Fort Drummond, a small earthwork built in 1814 for the positioning of cannon and gunpowder. A mound marking the remains of Fort Riall, a redoubt or small temporary fortification, can be seen close by. In 1906, the Lundy's Lane Historical Society erected a tablet on the northerly slope of

Queenston Heights restaurant, early 1900s

Queenston Heights Park to mark the site of the Redan Battery. All of the markers are included in the walking tour of the park.

Between Queenston and St. Davids on Highway 8A, still another marker notes the point at which General Sheaffe's men ascended the escarpment to defeat the entrenched enemy forces at the battle of Queenston Heights. Look for a grey stone on the south side of the Queenston-St. Davids road, 1½ miles west of Queenston.

ST. DAVIDS

Major David Secord, Laura's third son, received a land grant of 600 acres from the British Government as a Loyalist veteran of the American Revolution. On this grant, where two Indian trails intersected, he built a mill in 1786, with Four Mile Creek supplying the necessary water. His farm and mill prospered, eventually expanding into a milling centre for grist, lumber and flax. A tannery, distillery and furniture factory soon developed, with David becoming merchant and magistrate for the area as well. The village is thus named in his honor.

With the first rumblings of war in 1812, Major David Secord joined the fray again. While he was absent on duty in 1814, the small village was wantonly burned by American soldiers in retreat. The officer responsible was later court-martialled, but all of Major Secord's holdings were destroyed as well as most of the town. St. David's never again recovered its initial burst of energy.

David Secord's gravestone rests today, unembellished and forgotten, in the cemetery of St. Davids' United

Church (formerly Methodist) on the Queenston-St. Davids road near the main intersection of the village.

Historic buildings in town are few, but the aura of history lingers at its crossroads. Here at the main intersection in town stand a bank in a small white clapboard building, a general store from out of the past, a new Post Office and Fire Hall, a hardware store and gas station. On the northwest corner an old barn is all that is left of the blacksmith's shop, operated until 1945. On the northeast corner is the Presbyterian Church, a small red brick rectangle with Gothic windows, white trim and a white wooden door. It was once the headquarters of generals Derottenburg and Drummond during the War of 1812.

Across from the church on Pastor Lane, is a Georgian brick house, with an elaborate doorway with intricate fanlight and sidelights. It was built by the Woodruff family, who came to St. Davids at the same time as David Secord, and became equally prosperous as millers. They remained prominent in the area for generations, and descendants still reside in the family home.

The St. Davids Golf Course (262-4522), also on Paxton Lane, is renowned for its beauty, verging on an ancient escarpment, an historic cemetery, and overlooking rows of blossoming fruit trees in spring.

There is an antique shop called "Reflections in Tyme" on Highway 8, not far from St. Davids main intersection. It is housed in an old 2-storey white clapboard house with black trim and red doors. Only open by appointment in winter, and from 1 p.m. to 3 p.m., May 21st to the end of August, it specializes in antique brass beds. It also offers Canadiana, rocking chairs, pine tables and blanket chests and wooden washstands. (262-4405)

Canadian Canners is a fairly new addition to the area. Their plant here on Creek Road produces Aylmer and Del Monte brand fruits and vegetables, products of the same soil plowed by pioneers in the lovely orchards below.

On Highway 8, travelling towards Niagara Falls, the large, open Orchard Glen Market sells fresh produce. And farther still, on the same road, an old Indian burying ground is marked by a stone cairn at the side of the road.

VIRGIL

This settlement sprang up in the early 1800s around the junction of two roads cut through swamp and bush. Early inhabitants called the area "Marais Normand" or Norman Marsh. "The Crossroads," as the village came to be known, provided a convenient resting place for horses, just four miles from the village of Niagara-on-the-Lake, on the road to Toronto. It consisted of a few farms and a mill at the junction of Black Swamp Road (later Niagara Stone Road) and Four Mile Creek Road. Four Mile Creek, so named for its distance from Niagara-on-the-Lake, meandered through the bush on its way to empty into Lake Ontario to the north.

One early settler and farmer, George Lawrence, became an outstanding church leader in the tiny religious community and it soon took his name, Lawrenceville.

A hotel, no longer standing, flourished in the 1840s, catering to people traveling to Niagara. Population increased slowly and by 1862 the village was large enough to attract official attention. It was renamed Virgil, and its neighboring community, Homer, the reason for the classical names now unknown but probably chosen by a civic official with some interest in Latin and the Classics.

By this time Virgil could boast of two wagon makers, blacksmith shops, shoemakers and cabinet makers, as well as its hotel. None remain today. A few farm families flourished on its perimeter. Population remained constant, however, for many years.

At the end of the First World War, Virgil attracted a group of German Mennonite immigrants. Besides swelling the population of the settlement, these people proved to be hardworking, prosperous farmers. More arrived during the Depression and after the Second World War.

Virgil today is more than a simple crossroads, having become a vigorous, enterprising agricultural community. It boasts a modern district high school, a large medical clinic, several churches, a successful furniture industry and distribution centres for farm produce. On Niagara Stone Road, Brights Wines owns a large tract of vineyard for research and experimentation.

On Creek Road at the intersection of the Stone Road, the Virgil Baptist Church was built in 1841 and still stands, a simple white frame rectangle. When population dwindled in the 1930s, services were temporarily halted until the Russian-Ukrainian Baptists migrating to Virgil from Saskatchewan adopted the old building for their own use.

Also near the intersection, on Niagara Stone Road, the old St. John's Church, dating from 1894, is now a gift shop called "Periwinkle Place." It sells antiques, art, handcrafts and collectibles. Summers only. (468-2769)

Further along on Niagara Stone Road, towards Niagara, Wilson Johnson, woodcarver, displays his wares in a combined shop and studio. He creates beautiful reproductions of early Canadian pieces of furniture and decorative utensils used in settlers' homes. There is no telephone, but the shop is open six days a week summer and winter.

* * * * *

All three of these towns, Queenston, St. Davids and Virgil, share a common heritage. Their early settlements occurred along waterways which emptied into Lake Ontario; Queenston on the Niagara River, Virgil and St. Davids at Four Mile Creek. Ironically, the very reasons they were chosen — their marginal location, easy accessibility and proximity to water — were the reasons for their decline. With commerce moving to the Welland Canal, and government bodies moving to York (Toronto), their location became too marginal and their accessibility more difficult.

Today all three are incorporated into the town of Niagara-on-the-Lake, sharing memories and welcoming the suburban resident seeking peace and quiet.

Directory

EMERGENCY

Ambulance Service
St. Catharines Ambulance
688-2191

Drugs
Kennedy's Pharmacy
43 Queen Street
468-3238

Fire Emergency Calls
Niagara #1 Station
682-2453

Police
Niagara Regional Police
St. Catharines
688-4111

Hospital
Niagara Hospital
176 Wellington Street
468-3261

ARTISTS & CRAFTSMEN

Antique clock repair
John Kelly
123 William
468-7743

Artists, designers
Paul Johns, Ron Gordon
280 Dorchester
468-2724

Candle-makers
Peter Bolduc, Vickie Bolduc
510 Simcoe
Mar-Nic Crafts — Moffat Mews
468-3728

Clockmaker
Craig Lawson, "The Workshop"
Moffat Mews

Furniture refinishing
Ron Balasiuk
32 Castlereagh
468-7520

Hand weaving
Wilson Johnson
Niagara Stone Road
Virgil, Ontario

Interior designers
John Downton
Paul Firlotte
363 Simcoe
468-2760

Leather — custom work and repairs
Gary Jenney
212 Regent
468-3130

Needlepoint
Betty Mitchell
217 Butler
468-3120

Sculptor, etchings, engravings and woodcuts
Campbell Scott
89 Byron
468-3925

Wax miniatures — historical and haute couture
Dojji
Box 267
468-3101

BANKS

Bank of Montreal
91 Queen Street
468-3227

Canadian Imperial Bank of
  Commerce
27 Queen Street
468-3281

Royal Bank of Canada
Mississauga and Mary
468-3288

CHURCHES

Grace United
Victoria at Queen
no phone

Mennonite Brethren Church
Virgil
468-7155

Trinity Lutheran
Niagara Stone Road
468-2611

St. Andrew's Presbyterian
Simcoe Street
no phone

St. Mark's Anglican
41 Byron
468-3123

St. Vincent de Paul
73 Picton
468-7272

DRY CLEANER

Dreswell Dry Cleaner
126 Queen Street
468-3641

FLORISTS

Hurley's Flowers
124 Queen Street
468-3129

Van Noort Florists
Creek Road
468-7815

FOOD STORES

Becker's Milk
238 Mary Street
468-2354

Chambers Red and White Store
130 Queen Street
468-7731

McClelland's West End Store
106 Queen Street
468-7639

Pepe's Grocery and Gas Bar
242 Mary Street
468-3113

The Corner Store (Mac's Milk)
69 Queen Street
468-2512

The Fudge Shoppe
29 Queen Street
468-2593

The Theatre Deli
15 Queen Street
468-2296

HAIR STYLISTS

His and Hers Hairstyling
243 King Street
468-3506

House of Lords and Ladies
6 Picton Street
468-2219

Mr. Barry Hairstylist
125 Queen Street
468-2381

Eve Ormerod
238 Mary Street
468-2254

Regent Beauty Salon
516 Regent
468-7855

Stanley's Beauty Salon
431 Mississauga
468-3141

LIQUOR AND BEER

Brewers' Retail Store
284 Mary Street
468-3413

Liquor Control Board Outlet
20 Queen Street
468-3321

LOUNGES/BARS

American Hotel
61 Melville
468-3880

Riverside Hotel
35 Melville
468-7721

MORE RESTAURANTS

Alfredo's Pizzeria
245 King Street
468-7717

Stewart's Drive-In
390 Lakeshore
468-3557

The Old Town Ice Cream Shop
63 Queen Street
468-2532

SHOE REPAIR

Exclusive Leather
212 Regent
468-3130

TAXI, CAR RENTAL

Niagara Cab
280 King Street
468-3010

TRAVEL AGENTS

AJ's Travel
Moffat Mews
468-3980

Flarity Travel
20 King Street
St.Catharines
Call Barbara Evans, 468-7930

MISCELLANEOUS

Burland's Gifts
33 Queen Street
468-2524

Frontier Appliance
4 Queen Street
468-7292

Imperial Optical
188 Victoria
468-2455

Marianne's Fabrics
24 Picton
468-7808

Pauline's Fashion Shop
62 Queen Street
468-3500

Rolly's Jewellers
7 Queen Street
468-7233

Trivia
369 Mary Street
468-2574

Warren Heating & Plumbing
23 Queen Street
468-2127